Contents

Introduction

This book has been written using examples of species that are popular around the world. The techniques are not advanced, but are easily achievable by anyone who is prepared to attend workshops and classes. This book is designed to encourage rather than intimidate, and the author's aim is for the bonsai illustrated in this book to inspire and motivate the reader into becoming confident in their quest to create a bonsai or penjing. While the book looks at many species from all over the world, the basic techniques are explained in detail to help the bonsai-grower at all levels. If you are just starting bonsai, or have perhaps just one tree, then you will enjoy the great number of photo explanations showing ways in which to look after, or even create, your own bonsai.

A Short History of Bonsai

Although most people who are new to bonsai believe that it originated in Japan, bonsai actually started in China. However, popular bonsai, as we know it today, has been established by the Japanese and, indeed, many of the world's leading masters come from Japan.

In China, the art of miniaturizing trees is called penjing or pensai. The Chinese started to cultivate trees and shrubs in ceramic and wooden flowerpots, trays, and slabs of rock. They would also plant on deep-fissured, ornamental rocks. All of this started nearly two thousand years ago. One of the things noticeable about great civilizations is their interest in creating gardens. Most of us are familiar with the Willow Pattern plates that date from the 17th century, but the gardens that inspired them were already ancient by the time that Western eyes saw the

RIGHT This is an example of a white pine. Smaller examples are imported in their millions, and many can become as attractive as this one.

bonsai

for beginners

Dedication
*This book is dedicated to my wife, Svetlana Novikova Coussins,
a lover of old Russia, old poets, old writers, old songs, old singers,
old artists, old movies, and old movers.
She makes me feel younger every day.*

Craig Coussins

Sterling Publishing Co., Inc.
New York

for

beginners

Library of Congress
Cataloging-in-Publication Data Available

10 9 8 7 6 5 4 3 2 1

Published in 2001 by
Sterling Publishing Co., Inc.
387 Park Avenue South,
New York, NY 10016

First published in Great Britain by
D&S Books
Cottage Meadow,
Bocombe, Parkham,
Bideford,
Devon EX39 5PH

© 2000 D&S Books

Distributed in Canada by
Sterling Publishing
C/o Canadian Manda Group,
One Atlantic Avenue, Suite 105
Toronto, Ontario,
Canada M6K 3E7

Editorial Director: Sarah King
Editor: Sarah Harris
Project Editor: Clare Haworth-Maden
Designer: Axis Design

Sterling ISBN 0-8069-4031-X

splendors of the East. The tradition of Chinese gardening can be traced back almost 3500-thousand years. The Egyptians, and even the Persians, with their Hanging Gardens of Babylon, practiced this popular art. The Egyptians planted small trees in stone pockets around some of their most famous monuments, while the Bible refers to lands of lush vegetation and royal gardens where now only desert remains. The later, but still ancient, Arab nations loved their gardens, as can be seen in old Moorish palaces, such as the famous gardens in Granada.

Today you can see many Chinese gardens that have either been recreated according to the plans of ancient times or designed to emulate nature in miniature. This was the basis of the potted tree: to recreate in miniature a giant tree in the wild. Bonsai has not changed much since then.

The Chinese have written many books on horticulture. As far back as AD 500, the uses of air-layering, grafting, and seed propagation were written about. In the ancient Gardens of Xian, home of the famous terracotta warriors, sits one of my own trees. Collected on a Scottish mountain peak in 1978, it was designed in the southern Chinese Penjing style and was presented to the people of Xian by its twin city, Edinburgh. I suggested this as a sign of respect for China's ancient tradition of penjing, as well as bringing the younger, Western understanding of the art to China.

ABOVE Windswept trees form part of our dictionary of bonsai styles. We can easily recreate this image and, like a painting, it, too, reminds us of nature, freedom, open spaces, mountains, and landscapes. And we escape for a few minutes into the illusion that we have created ourselves. That is the beauty of bonsai and the earliest reason that bonsai were first grown.

ABOVE The Xian pine tree two years after collection and in its second year of styling, 1984.

ABOVE RIGHT After four years of styling the Xian pine was not ready, but we had run out of time and the tree had to start traveling. The pot is a Japanese drum pot.

The Hobby Today

What happened to penjing? The early traders between Japan and China brought these little trees, rocks, and plants back home, where they were collected by both wealthy merchants and samurai. In the process, the word pensai became bonsai, which has the same meaning – a tree in a tray. Penjing is the Chinese name for this kind of art form, while bonsai is the Japanese. The samurai loved art, nature, and meditation. It was part of their inherent culture.

Real trade did not take place into Japan until the 16th and 17th centuries, but soon the Japanese started developing their own bonsai. The Chinese had already laid down about thirty different styles of tree, covering the five major regions of China at that time, and the Japanese accepted and developed them. Bonsai, as we know it today, however, really started within the last fifty years, as can be determined from the quality of trees in past exhibitions. Something changed at that time. Before then, the clip-and-grow method, tying with strings, and pruning to shape, were the main methods of styling the bonsai or penjing. Indeed, many countries in Asia other than Japan still use the clip-and-grow method. Ancient Japanese gardens featured expertly pruned garden trees, and the techniques learned from these had been applied to bonsai. The reason why things changed in Japan was the advent of copper wire. Wire was freely available after the war and many gardeners started to recover old trees that had been abandoned during World War II. Wire was the new string – the new styling material. Some growers had certainly experimented with wire before, but it was the easy availability of this material that now made wire popular.

Bonsai and penjing are art forms. A good bonsai is one that resembles a real tree in style and perspective. Age, size, and trunk widths are not the most important aspects of bonsai. The viewer should see a full-sized tree in miniature and growing in its natural environment. If it looks like a real tree, then the bonsai has succeeded. It is, of course, an illusion.

So why was the use of copper wire such a major development? The main advantage of wire was that it was now possible to style the tree by wrapping wire around all of the branches, twigs, and trunk, and to bend and shape these in any way. The relative success of the outcome, however, depended on the enthusiast being artistic enough to know which way these branches needed to be bent and also having enough horticultural knowledge not to kill the tree in the process.

Over the period from 1950 through to the early 1960s the use of wire and new, fast-growing techniques had resulted in some wonderful trees being developed, and when the hobby reached the West during the early 1960s some superb-quality trees were being exported in their hundreds. Unfortunately, many of these early trees were killed by ignorance. In general, they were expensive presents given to people who invariably had little clue as to how to look after them. At this time the market for bonsai was small and relatively obscure. It took the growing interest of bonsai clubs to develop the hobby. In North America, bonsai as a hobby slowly gained popularity during the late 1960s through teachers such as John Yoshio Naka, while in Europe the teachings of Peter Adams helped it to take off during the late 1970s. By the mid-1980s, Europe had a scattering of bonsai clubs, and by the late 1990s some of the finest bonsai artists came from all over the world. It was no longer just a Chinese or Japanese hobby. The world's best bonsai

BELOW Exquisite Japanese gardens in Brooklyn Botanic Gardens, New York.

artists, such as Kimura, were still in Japan, but they were now traveling and teaching at international conventions. Today we have incredible bonsai artists from Europe and North America, as well as Asia. The hobby has come of age in the new millennium.

As the hobby has grown, it has encompassed enthusiasts from all occupations. Fellow club-members may include a surgeon or a market trader, a homemaker, or a lawyer. There are no class barriers to bonsai, and everyone can grow or buy their own. Clubs are the best way in which to learn the hobby on a practical level, but this book will teach you the basics and you can continue to use it as your main reference for many years.

At the turn of the century, there were over 100,000 enthusiasts in Britain and 250,000 in the United States (these figures are based on sales of bonsai across those two countries).

ABOVE Another beautiful Japanese garden in Brooklyn Botanic Garden.

RIGHT A Korean hornbeam (*Carpinus turkzaninowii*). Hornbeams are deciduous trees that can be identified by their pear-shaped leaves with serrated edges and their shadow-striped trunks.

RIGHT A fine example of a miniature elm in summer. It is 1m (40") tall.

BELOW Ezo (Yezo) spruce (*Picea jezoensis*).

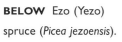

BELOW The strangely contorted shape of a collected Scots pine.

Choosing Your Bonsai

On a philosophical level, the appearance of a finely twigged, deciduous bonsai, or a dense pine, can promote a feeling of peace. Bonsai arose from the art of meditation, and, as you will soon come to realize when attending to your bonsai, time quickly passes when you are working on these little trees. Some people keep bonsai as art objects in their living spaces, while others just like the idea of making a miniature tree.

ABOVE A money tree *(Crassula)* is a good indoor tree for bonsai enthusiasts, as the leaves can be pruned to the first set of new leaves throughout the year. It takes about four years to achieve a nice tree shape, and the bonsai will look great throughout the year. If you do not cut, then you will not get the tight growth that the *Crassula* is capable of.

Beginners, or less experienced growers, are concerned in the first year with the accumulation of either material or knowledge. The former often get themselves into a situation in which they have too many trees, and subsequently few, if any, of these trees receive individual attention. This kind of enthusiast usually has far too many things in pots *(potensai)* and not enough time to nurture and cultivate them into bonsai, so he or she often spends money on imported stock that looks the part.

The other enthusiast tries to maintain a small selection of trees that allows them to try out the different techniques that they have learned from books written by experienced bonsai-growers. The downside of accumulating too much information is that the enthusiast can often prefer the knowledge to actually practicing the hobby.

BELOW A healthy example of a fig *(Ficus)*.

ABOVE When you see a bonsai, does it remind you of a full-sized tree? This is an excellent cypress *(Chamaecyparis obtusa nana gracilis)*. It looks like a real tree and fulfills all of the requirements for a nice bonsai.

ABOVE This stump fig (*Ficus*) is typical of the poor material that is often offered. It is easy to work with, but will take about four years to develop a nice branch shape.

BELOW Seeing a tree in nature can inspire you to create a similar tree in miniature.

ABOVE This is a large Chinese elm (*Ulmus parviflora*). It is ready for trimming on foliage pads. These trees are very easy to look after.

Bonsai or penjing?

The difference between bonsai and penjing is not something that a beginner is generally aware of. The majority of little bonsai – elms, *Serissa* etc. – are from Taiwan, China, Formosa, Vietnam, and many other Asian countries. These have been grown in the clip-and-grow style, which was the principal styling method of Chinese bonsai. It involves pruning and developing secondary buds, which then develop into branch areas. These branches have been trained by using string and weights, but rarely, if ever, wire. Some can be

ABOVE An Asian black pine (*Pinus thunbergii*). While not the best example of a penjing, this looser-style bonsai is more penjing in nature – almost destructured and natural. These qualities are more Chinese than Japanese.

ABOVE RIGHT This Asian black pine (*Pinus thunbergii*) has a more structured style that is generally associated with classical bonsai.

FAR RIGHT This bonsai is less than 1m (40") tall. It is a needle juniper (*Juniperus rigida*).

very nice, but most are just little trunks with a few twigs set into a small pot and sold to the West as bonsai. Such trees will take a lot of care from their owner – and direction from this book – to help them to become a bonsai, or a penjing.

For the majority of people, the terms bonsai and penjing are synonymous. Bonsai is a more structured form of growing, although we now have so many styles that it is hard to determine what is, and what is not, bonsai. The pictures in this book should give you a good understanding of what a bonsai should look like.

Which species to start with

The best species to choose largely depends on whether you live in the northern or southern hemisphere. Refer to the Bonsai Quick-reference Table at the end of the book.

Popular outdoor species in temperate areas of the globe, such as the northern U.S., Canada and northern Europe, parts of South Africa, New Zealand (South Island), Japan, and other temperate areas of Asia, include junipers (*Juniperus*), pines (*Pinus*), maples (*Acer*), larches (*Larix*), cotoneasters (*Cotoneaster*), hemlocks (*Tsuga*), oaks (*Quercus*), and beeches (*Fagus*). There are also many local species that have their own particular requirements. In the U.S. these

include buttonwoods (*Conocarpus*), cypresses (*Taxodium*), and desert junipers (*Juniperus*). South Africa has acacias, white olives (*Buddleja*), peaches (*Kiggelaria*), and figs (*Ficus*). Australia also has figs, as well as gums (*Eucalyptus*), while New Zealand has Totaras, Pohutukawas and Rimus. Local climatic differences will determine the species used.

For complete beginners, cotoneasters are

almost impossible to kill, and cypresses, such as the *Chamaecyparis pissifera*, are very easy to develop. Maples are excellent, except that you must keep them out of frosts, but conversely they are also temperate species, and conifers, pines, larches, cedars etc. are sometimes a little slow to grow. Elms *(Ulmus)* and zelkovas are excellent for bonsai, and can be grown almost anywhere in the world because there are so many varieties of indoor and outdoor elms these days. Any of the indoor species used in temperate climates, such as sageretia, serisa, and Chinese elms, are also very easy to grow. It is a good idea to find species that are quick-growing, so that you can see a result, or else growing a bonsai could end up like watching paint dry.

Seed culture is also extremely slow, and in my opinion should only be tried in addition to other methods. Buying a bonsai is easy, and is the usual route into the hobby, but only buy a tree that is workable. Avoid pines to start with, as they can be slow to develop if you are a beginner. A maple, juniper, or cypress will be an excellent first tree as they are all vigorous plants.

In colder climates, the indoor varieties consist of tropical trees. These include figs, a succulent known as the money tree (*Crassula*), sageritia, serissa. and many other species. Sold in millions from department stores, nurseries, and market stalls, their life span is invariably short because many are bought as gifts and are given to people who do not have the knowledge or inclination to care for them.

RIGHT Look for good balance. This is evident in this trident maple, with the roots over rock. Good branch structure or ramification with dense twigs.

Indoor Trees

Indoor trees are becoming more popular with beginners in temperate climates. These bonsai are tropical trees that need to be kept indoors in colder parts of the world, although they can be put outside in summer. They should be fertilized every two weeks throughout the year with high nitrogen in the spring, balanced in the summer, and low, tomato, or 0-10-10 (fully explained in the feeding section), in the fall. Use at half strength in the spring and full strength in summer.

Before beginning your hobby, it is important to determine which kind of bonsai you want, or wish to own – indoor or outdoor? When buying bonsai, it is worth going to a specialist nursery, where you can be sure of getting only good-quality trees and the staff will also provide helpful instructions and advice. Even many nurseries specializing outdoor trees have bowed to the knowledge that indoor trees are becoming much more popular these days (especially during the festive period), and will generally have everything that you need. The following growing details apply to all houseplants.

ABOVE Serisa leaves.

ABOVE A close-up of carmona leaves.

Placement For Indoor Trees

Place indoor trees in a bright window, but do not shut the curtains over them at night, as this will chill them too much. It is important to be aware that these are essentially tropical trees – hence their indoor status – and that they need some heat. Normal room temperature will suffice in most cases. You can put your indoor tree outside in the summer, but bring it in when the nights start to become cold.

RIGHT This is a good specimen of a carmona with a twin trunk grown in the penjing style.

FAR RIGHT Serisa is a twiggy species, and many nurseries offer this kind of material.

Light

You must turn the trees around a half-turn every week to allow an even distribution of light. This will prevent the tree from dying on one side.

Watering

Keep the soil slightly damp in winter and do not allow it to dry out. Check the soil every two days. Take the bonsai into the bathroom every day and spray it gently with a very light mister or misting bottle filled with water (as used by hairdressers). Do not sit the tree directly in a dish of water. You can, however, place some small stones in a dish or a flat container, pour water into the dish just below the surface of the stones, place the tree on top and allow the water to evaporate upward. This benefits the tree. Water it more often in spring and summer, usually every day.

Feeding

Indoor bonsai can take a ready-bought plant food every week. Outdoor bonsai will take half-strength high nitrogen in spring every two weeks, and tomato or zero nitrogen, such as 0-10-10, in late summer through to the beginning of leaf

Beginner's Tips

Bonsai need watering. They are not ornaments. They need food to grow and thrive. Prune them if they need it. Their small size is deceptive — they are not as fragile as they look. If your tree has lost all of its leaves, it has probably been frosted, or chilled, and is going dormant. If this happens, place it in a cool room. A dark room is best, but some light is not harmful. The tree will flourish again in the spring. However, check if the twigs and branchlets are shriveled. If so, the tree has died. If you have recently bought the tree from a reputable dealer, return it. As long as you have been following the instructions carefully, a healthy bonsai should thrive. If it did not survive for a reasonable time after following the instructions for care, then you were sold a dead or dying tree. Get it replaced.

BELOW Bonsai for sale on benches.

RIGHT A nursery display
bench of different heights
that can be viewed from
both sides. Much stock can
be displayed on this type of
unit.

RIGHT This is a black
pine (*Pinus thunbergii*). You
will only see a good-quality
specimen like this in good
nurseries.

change in fall, or in late fall in the case of
evergreens such as pines.

Pruning and Shaping

Leafy bonsai will soon grow to length, so trim
them back to above the first set of new growth at
the top, the second set around the sides in the
middle area, and the third set around the sides at
the bottom. The plant will soon form into a
recognizable tree shape.

Buying from Nurseries and Garden Centers

The first important point to remember is always
to buy from a reputable dealer. Bonsai can often
be found at country fairs and garage sales at
tempting prices, but be wary. Not only will you
have no idea if the tree is in good condition, or
even properly labeled, but you will not have the
nursery's support system if anything goes wrong.

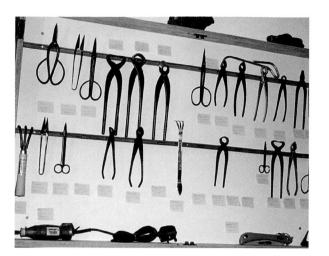

ABOVE A selection of the many tools that are available to bonsai-growers.

It is not unknown for the unscrupulous to use these outlets to dispose of stolen plants! It is therefore important always to buy from a specialist supplier.

When buying your bonsai, there are many questions that you should ask to enable you to care for and maintain a healthy tree.

● What conditions does the tree need?
● What aftercare does it require and what guarantees does the seller give if the tree dies within the first few months? (Ask for this information to be written down before you agree to purchase the bonsai.)
● What after-sales service does the supplier offer in the way of repotting, winter care, holiday care etc?
● Get a proper, detailed receipt.

Check that the soil does not consist of clay mud. Professional growers would have removed this soil and would have replaced it with soil more suited to local conditions.

Aftercare

Make sure that you have read about, or listened carefully to, the requirements of your new bonsai. Some general points: keep the bonsai out of extreme weather conditions – wind, rain, sun, and centrally heated homes. Most trees die within a few weeks if they are not kept correctly, and yet the trees really require very little in the way of pampering. Keep the tree in a slightly shaded place and spray it lightly every day for the first two weeks. Do not feed it immediately, but wait until the tree has settled down. The problem with immediate feeding is that the tree may have been repotted recently and its roots freshly cut; if you feed it too quickly, you may harm the roots. Find out when the tree was last repotted and explain why you need this information. If you cannot be certain, then it is best to withhold feeding for about six weeks. After a couple of weeks, give the tree about four hours of sunlight per day, but still find a place away from high winds. If you receive, or buy, an outdoor tree in the winter, do not bring the bonsai into a centrally heated house, as this will aggravate the tree's normal growing period, exhausting it and drying up the foliage.

Tools

Tools are acquired as you progress as a beginner, and after three months you will probably have everything that you need. Any bonsai nursery will advise you on your basic requirements. All you need to start with are an angle-cutter, a knob-cutter, a pair of sharp bonsai scissors, and jinning pliers. Other "toys" can be added later. I have hundreds of tools, but my working set really only consists of these four items.

BELOW This magnificent landscape planting is in the Marbella Bonsai Museum and Nursery in Spain. It measures 2m (80").

What to Look For When Buying a Bonsai

The first thing to look for when buying a bonsai is if all the stock throughout the store is looking fresh. In the case of white pine, are the needles healthy and "crisp green," or are they brown-tinged and looking dejected? Are all of the trees on show in clean pots, or are they in dirty, unkempt containers? Is the soil damp or very dry? If the soil is damp, check that the needles are not brown from overwatering. If the soil is very dry, look closely at the needles and twigs to see if they are dried up and wrinkled – a sign of dehydration. Do not buy a pine that has deep wire marks or where any wire left on is biting into the bark. This will rarely, if ever, grow out of most trees, and certainly not pines. Buying any tree with wire marks is a sign of poor training and can be a difficult thing to correct.

In addition, make sure that there are instructions with the tree, that you get a receipt, and that the seller is prepared to exchange the

RIGHT A nicely styled white pine (*Pinus parviflora*).

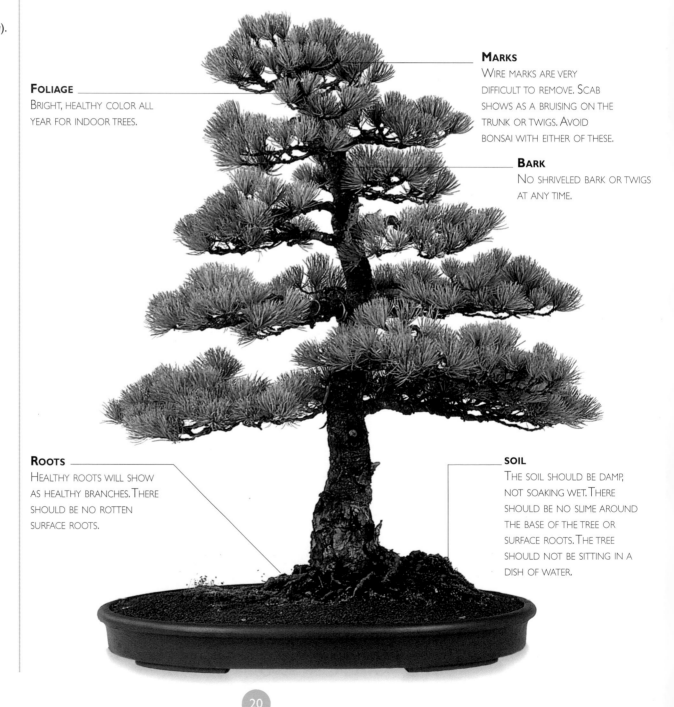

FOLIAGE
BRIGHT, HEALTHY COLOR ALL YEAR FOR INDOOR TREES.

MARKS
WIRE MARKS ARE VERY DIFFICULT TO REMOVE. SCAB SHOWS AS A BRUISING ON THE TRUNK OR TWIGS. AVOID BONSAI WITH EITHER OF THESE.

BARK
NO SHRIVELED BARK OR TWIGS AT ANY TIME.

ROOTS
HEALTHY ROOTS WILL SHOW AS HEALTHY BRANCHES. THERE SHOULD BE NO ROTTEN SURFACE ROOTS.

SOIL
THE SOIL SHOULD BE DAMP, NOT SOAKING WET. THERE SHOULD BE NO SLIME AROUND THE BASE OF THE TREE OR SURFACE ROOTS. THE TREE SHOULD NOT BE SITTING IN A DISH OF WATER.

tree should you have followed all of the instructions, but the tree still dies.

You may be tempted to buy a seed kit, but these should be avoided. There is no such thing as a bonsai seed. You are simply buying a tree seed, which will take many, many years to grow to the stature represented by the picture on the packet. It is far better to buy a seedling if you want to watch your plant grow from its earliest beginnings.

FOLIAGE
BRIGHT, HEALTHY COLOR FROM SPRING THOUGH FALL FOR OUTDOOR TREES.

BARK
THE BARK SHOULD BE IN GOOD CONDITION ALL YEAR FOR BOTH INDOOR AND OUTDOOR TREES.

ROOTS
THE TREE SHOULD NOT MOVE IN THE POT — GENTLY TRY TO MOVE IT TO SEE IF IT DOES (SEE SOIL).

BELOW A beech in winter is as attractive as it is in summer, but make sure that any winter foliage is nowhere to be seen in summer!

Caring For Your Bonsai

Bonsai are grown in shallow pots, and because of this certain factors will affect the growth. The roots quickly fill up the available space and they need nourishment in the form of water, as well as fertilizer. Shallow pots dry out quickly, so you must think about bonsai needs. Tiny bonsai will need more water, while large bonsai may need a little less. Never direct a sprinkler into the soil of a bonsai pot, as that may wash the soil away. Always use watering cans with a fine rose.

BELOW If you intend to use a watering can, try to get a long-necked one because it is easier to apply to relatively small pots. Turn the rose or cap upside down and then water. This gives the force of light rain on the plants. Long-necked watering cans are also excellent for getting into crowded winter storage areas when you only want to water a specific plant as opposed to all of them.

Watering outdoor plants

The tree needs water to survive and the water should be soft. If you do not have soft water, then store your water supply in a large container such as a rain barrel. It is best to use the water from the top of the barrel. If you have a faucet, then place it at least 20cm (8") above the bottom. Limescale deposits can then sink to the bottom and settle as sludge, which you should siphon out now and again with a hose. A tried-and-tested method is to fill a rain barrel, drop in a mesh bag of peat, and leave it for two weeks before using the water on your plants. Drop a little insecticide into the barrel to kill the mosquito colonies that will inevitably appear unless the lid is a tight fit. If your area has problems with water quality, however, do not worry too much about it. Just let the water settle for a day in your watering can and any heavy material should drop to the bottom. Then wash out the can.

Hard or limescaled water can affect some plants. Direct the water from your guttering into a barrel and when it is full cut off that supply until it is required again. Use a long-necked watering can with a fine rose at the end, because this allows the water to fall softly like rain. Watering should be done in the evening, so that the bonsai can absorb water overnight. In warmer weather, water in the morning as well, to give the bonsai some moisture during the day. In really hot weather, you may have to water three times a day. Avoid spraying the leaves with water during hot, sunny days, as that can damage the leaves.

As well as following these guidelines, use your common sense to determine the watering regime. Essentially, in the summer, water twice a day.

Automatic watering systems are fine if you have a lot of bonsai, but you must still check that each pot is actually receiving water. Using automatic systems in hard-water areas directly from the faucet can harm some species, so check before using them. For example, do not use them on lime-hating plants, such as azaleas.

Spraying or misting the leaves will emulate a drenching of rain. This is necessary to stop the leaves from drying up. It is especially important that you spray junipers and needle bonsai. Use either a hand-sprayer or a heavy-duty one if you have a number of bonsai. You can add the correct fertilizer to the misting water every two weeks to administer a foliar feed.

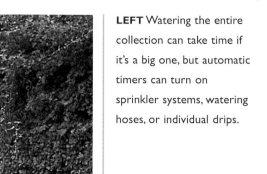

LEFT Watering the entire collection can take time if it's a big one, but automatic timers can turn on sprinkler systems, watering hoses, or individual drips.

WATERING CHART

SPRING	SUMMER	FALL	WINTER

EARLY SPRING
CONIFERS / EVERGREENS Once or twice a week.

DECIDUOUS After bud starts to swell, water once or twice a week.

LATE SPRING
CONIFERS / EVERGREENS Twice a week. Mist.

DECIDUOUS Twice a week, but in warmer weather every two days.

EARLY SUMMER
CONIFERS / EVERGREENS Every day. Mist.

DECIDUOUS Every day, but in hot weather up to twice a day. Mist.

MIDSUMMER
CONIFERS / EVERGREENS Once or twice a day. Mist.

DECIDUOUS Twice a day, early morning and evening. Mist.

FALL
CONIFERS / EVERGREENS Every two or three days.

DECIDUOUS Every two days. If the leaves have fallen off, then keep damp.

EARLY WINTER
CONIFERS / EVERGREENS Once a week. Keep damp.

DECIDUOUS Keep damp.

WINTER
CONIFERS / EVERGREENS Keep slightly damp.

DECIDUOUS If not in leaf, just keep slightly damp.

LATE WINTER
CONIFERS / EVERGREENS Once a week to keep damp.

DECIDUOUS Watch for buds before watering. Keep damp.

RIGHT Keep deciduous trees, like this birch (*Betula*), slightly damp in the winter.

RIGHT Spray needle foliage two or three times a day during the growing season. This is a *Chamaecyparis obtusa*.

Watering Indoor Plants

Generally, water bonsai every two or three days if they are kept inside, but in winter just keep the soil damp. Do not overwater, as the tree's transpiration rate may not be fast enough to take in all of the moisture and the roots may start to rot. Always mist your indoor bonsai, as humidity levels need to be maintained. It is a good idea to put indoor trees outside in the summer, but water them normally, as shown in the chart on page 23.

Watering indoor trees really means keeping the soil damp. One method of doing this is to place pebbles in a watertight tray. Fill the tray with water to just below the top of the pebbles and sit the bonsai pot on top. As the water evaporates it acts as a constantly rising mist in a warm house (see light and placement of indoor trees).

Vacation Time

It is vital to ensure that your bonsai receive proper attention while you are on vacation. If you ask a neighbor or relative to water them when you are away, make sure that they have been with you at least twice for a watering session; that they have been fully briefed as to what is required; and let them water under your watchful eye. Too many bonsai have been killed by garden-hose jets being turned on full and then either blasting all of the soil out of the pot or washing the pot off the shelf. You cannot expect someone who has no experience to care for your bonsai correctly. Allow sufficient time for a few training sessions in order to reassure them – and yourself – that they know what they are doing.

If you have expensive bonsai, then it may be better either to house them with another bonsai enthusiast or to ask your local bonsai nursery to look after them, although you will usually have to pay for this. Look at their own watering systems first, however, because some nurseries pay scant attention to other people's trees. Always insist on a written receipt for your tree, as it is not unknown for private bonsai to have been accidentally sold as the nursery's stock.

Light and Placement

It is very important to understand all of the bonsai's requirements. Light and placement are particularly important. For example, if you grow a maple in the shade, the internodes (the distance between each set of leaves) will be very long. If you grow the maple in full sunlight, then these internodes will be very short. As it is preferable to have a tight growth on a bonsai, plenty of light is needed to get the best result from your maple. However, too much sunlight will cause the tree to dry out too quickly and the leaves may scorch in the sun. There is a fine balance between too

much, and too little, light.

If it is to thrive, a bonsai needs a bit of both sunlight and shade. Some shade is good in the summer, as long as the tree gets some sun. This is when the placement of the tree is important.

When placing your bonsai, you need to think about when and where the sun is going to shine. You should ensure that your tree receives around four hours of full sun a day. If you build a shade

LEFT Light and shade dance in this exquisite white pine (*Pinus parviflora*), which has been trained in the cascade style. The pot is a Chinese antique.

LEFT Overhanging branches shading part of a crystal pool. When placing your bonsai on a bench at home, remember to ensure that the smaller trees are not shaded by larger branches or full-sized trees around your garden. This can be a problem in apartments where window boxes are being used. The sides may be high enough to give protection from wind, but may also block side light.

RIGHT Outdoor bonsai
that are kept in apartments
can be placed outside in
purpose-built window
boxes like this one.

section, make sure that it does not cover the tree all day. In hot climates, you may often find entire collections covered with fine, plastic mesh to help shade the trees. If you employ this method, ensure that all of the trees are moved around regularly to enable an even distribution of light.

Even if you have only one bonsai, make sure that you turn the tree round a quarter-turn each day, or, at the least, turn it round a half-turn each week to ensure that the foliage receives light evenly. If you do not do this, then the tree will die on the side that remains out of the light. The most effective method is to move all of your trees at the same time. Put a marker at the front of each bonsai and leave it there. Every time you turn the bonsai, all of the markers should be in the same place. In this way, if you overlook one, it is easy to spot the out-of-line marker.

Pines and junipers will have different colors of foliage, depending on the light. Many pines or junipers will develop a bluish tone to their needles if kept in shade, but if kept in full sun

they will become slightly more yellowish. The ideal solution, of course, is a mixture of sun and shade. I prefer to give my trees early-day or late-afternoon sun, and shade in the middle of the day. It is up to you to plan your display area.

One very simple idea is to move the tree or trees around their shelf area every week. As long as they are small, this presents no problem. When your trees start to become bigger, however, it will be impossible. Bigger trees need to be permanently placed on turntables.

In tropical climates, where the sun is strong, many trees are used to high temperatures. In order to keep your trees alive, however, you must still try to keep them out of the strong midday sun. In this case, misting the trees up to three or four times a day will help the bonsai or penjing by increasing the humidity levels and therefore reducing their transpiration rates.

Wind is also a factor that many new growers are unaware of. When a tree starts to produce foliage in the spring, the leaves can be very soft.

Wind, which is common at this time of year, can cause havoc with these soft, lush leaves. Protect the tree from direct wind at this time and, indeed, at all times, if possible. In some cities around the world the wind never ceases, and growers have to build windbreaks around their bonsai area. The best windbreak is a commercial, plastic break, with specially cut holes in the structure to dissipate the force of the wind. Used extensively by professional plant nurseries, this material is readily available to buy. It normally comes in rolls 2m (6½ft) in length, and between 5 and 20m (16½ and 66½ft) long. Support it between solid, square fence posts that have been well anchored into the ground. One solution is to build a pergola and to tack the mesh to it on three sides. Use the fourth side for winter.

Another good placement are window boxes that are high enough to protect the sides of the bonsai, but large enough to give it enough light. This is an ideal solution if you live in an apartment, although be considerate if you have neighbors downstairs. Be careful when watering your bonsai, as they may not appreciate muddy drips of water on their windows!

Light and Placement of Indoor Trees

Indoor trees should be turned around every day. The light levels are very important. Do not keep bonsai in a window through which the sun can shine and dry up or burn them.

Avoid placing your bonsai on top of electrical equipment, such as televisions, as the combination of water and electric current could have shocking results – literally.

LEFT A selection of miniature maple (*Acer*) bonsai. The smallest is 10cm (4") high.

Temperature

Do not keep bonsai in a window where the curtains are closed on them each night, as the cold area between the curtain and the bonsai may chill the trees and cause them to die. Bathrooms are good, as long as the bathroom does not become too cold when it is not in use.

Avoid placing bonsai near electric fires or real fires, too. Humidity is important, and you can maintain that by misting the bonsai with a hand-mister. Reduce the misting in the winter, however, as the tree growth may slow down if it does not actually go into dormancy.

The temperature of the indoor bonsai should remain constant during much of the year – as for any house plant. The only exception is that some trees start dropping leaves slightly, signaling the advent of the tree's winter. If that starts to happen, place the tree in a cool room, but do not let it become too cold. In particular, avoid exposing it to frost or cold weather. The tree will pick up again in the spring. The dormancy of an indoor tree should not be confused with a dying tree. A dead or dying tree can usually be identified by closely examining the bark and branches. If these are slightly shriveled, then the tree is in trouble. It has either been overwatered

ABOVE Fukien tea (*Carmona*), from tropical, Asian areas, is a good indoor tree in colder climates. The leaves are small, glossy, and dark-green in color.

RIGHT Chinese elm has a softer color than *Carmona*. Often kept in the home in colder climates, the use of a white tray allows light to be reflected onto the tree.

Perching it on a shelf away from any light will cause the tree to die, so keep it in a light position near a window, like any other house plant, and display it anywhere you want when you have visitors, but make sure that you put it back near a window for good light. Avoid exposing it to full sun for long periods.

If you want to use more advanced light-management techniques for indoor plants, then you caould use the truelight/natural-light fluorescent tubes designed for terrariums. These give out 95 percent natural light as opposed to normal fluorescent lights that give out 40 percent natural light. This is good for dark apartments or houses. If you use one, then display your bonsai or penjing like a fish tank. Indeed, as long as it is not allowed to become damp and cold, you can display small bonsai in an empty aquarium.

or underwatered. Otherwise, it could have been left in a cold window with the curtains closed (see Troubleshooting).

Temperature and the Outdoor Bonsai

It is not wise to bring outdoor trees inside during their dormant period, as that may start them growing prior to their normal development. Dormancy is signaled by the leaves dropping from deciduous trees. Pines and junipers

also go into a semidormant state during this period, and in extremely cold climates all trees simply stop growing. It is necessary to protect them from frost, wind, and other forms of bad weather, so store them in a shed or an unheated garage. Evergreens need some light, but deciduous trees need very little. A cold greenhouse may not be ideal, as it may heat up on sunny winter days unless shaded. The same goes for glass porches or conservatories.

BELOW This is a maple (*Acer palmatum kashima*) group, which is also known as a multiple-trunk style. Note the well-shaped foliage pads.

Keeping Your Bonsai Healthy

The previous chapter looked at ways of caring for your bonsai in terms of watering, placement, and temperature. However, there are two further factors to consider, and these are feeding and pest control. Providing the correct balance of feed for your miniature tree is very important, as is vigilance in checking for, and eliminating, pests and diseases. Some common care dilemmas are also dealt with in a troubleshooting guide at the end of this chapter.

Feeding

In general, every two weeks feed bonsai with a high-nitrogen fertilizer from late spring, and then in summer feed them with a balanced fertilizer, stopping for four weeks during the hottest part of summer and starting again in late summer with a low-nitrogen or tomato fertilizer. High-nitrogen fertilizer feeds leaves and buds, and low-nitrogen fertilizer feeds twigs, roots, trunks, and branches.

Spray bonsai with a foliar feed every two weeks in spring, and mist the foliage with water in warm weather to keep the humidity levels up.

To avoid lush or soft growth initially, such as in pines or maples, use a zero-based nitrogen fertilizer, 0-10-10, or, at the worse, a low-nitrogen fertilizer, such as tomato fertilizer, at the beginning of the season. To get a bright fall color in maples, do not feed them more than twice during the entire season.

It is important to remember that using liquid feeds allows the food to pass quickly through the soil, and if your soil is correct, then some will be retained during the feeding process. While watering during rain is sometimes unavoidable,

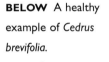

BELOW A healthy example of *Cedrus brevifolia.*

When Not to Feed

● DO NOT FEED DECIDUOUS TREES BEFORE BUD BREAK

● DO NOT FEED IN WINTER, BECAUSE TREES CANNOT ABSORB THE FEED

● DO NOT FEED SICK TREES, AS THEY WILL NOT BE ABLE TO ABSORB THE NUTRIENTS EASILY

● DO NOT FEED AFTER REPOTTING FOR AT LEAST SIX TO EIGHT WEEKS, AS ROOTS ARE TOO DELICATE AND WILL BE DAMAGED

ABOVE Pellet feeds can include rapeseed cake or, in this case, a Japanese product called Bio Gold, now sold in bonsai nurseries all over the world.

soil- and foliar-feeding of bonsai with large canopies of foliage during rain is not a good idea, as the water will wash through the soil much faster. Small trees can be immersed in a bucket or sink filled with feed, and when the bubbles stop rising the tree will have received sufficient food and water. Do not do this every day if you have outdoor trees. On the other hand, it may well be the only available method for an indoor tree (if you live in an apartment, for example). In that case, you will probably find that your tree will only need watering once or twice a week and feeding once every two weeks.

BELOW This chart has been created as a guideline only. In some countries, the summer lasts longer than two to four weeks, and feeding during this time may also have the effect of accidentally concentrating the fertilizer due to quick evaporation.

Feeding Chart DETAILED FEEDING REGIME. HIGH NITROGEN MEANS REGULAR PLANT FOOD AND NOT LAWN FOOD.

PERIOD	VERY YOUNG TREES	TREES IN TRAINING	ESTABLISHED TREES
WINTER DORMANCY	No feed.	No feed.	No feed.
EARLY SPRING At bud break wait until the leaf has fully opened before feeding.	Start feeding high-nitrogen fertilizer at half strength. Feed every week.	To avoid lush growth, feed a zero nitrogen fertilizer, such as 0-10-10, or tomato fertilizer at worse. Feed for two weeks at half strength.	Zero-nitrogen feed once in early spring.
LATE SPRING Leaves are now fully developed and candles are swelling on pines. Protect from winds, as the leaves are soft.	Feed at half strength every week. Increase to full strength at the end of this period.	Continue to feed every two weeks, but now start introducing high-nitrogen fertilizer.	Feed once with high-nitrogen fertilizer at half strength.
EARLY SUMMER Leaves are now firming up, so continue with feeding. Protect from pests.	Increase to full-strength high-nitrogen fertilizer every week. Use a balanced fertilizer toward the end of this period.	Use a balanced fertilizer at half strength every three weeks. Or start to use slow-release cake fertilizer. Maples, elms, and zelkovas need less feed but more pinching, to develop fine twigs.	One feed of high-nitrogen fertilizer and a plant tonic during this period. Do not overfeed established trees, as they will grow to length.
MIDSUMMER The tree enters a semidormant period at this stage, so it is wiser to stop feeding for between two and four weeks.	Stop feed.	Stop feed.	Stop feed.
LATE SUMMER This is the period prior to leaf change, but after the heat of mid-summer.	Start using a low-nitrogen fertilizer every week at full strength. Use a foliar feed as well each week.	Start using a low-nitrogen fertilizer every three weeks at full strength. Foliar feed at the same time.	Two applications of low-nitrogen fertilizer or, even better, 0-10-10, during this period. Foliar feed once.
FALL Leaf change heralds the onset of dormancy in deciduous trees.	Stop feeding when leaves start to change, Keep feeding evergreens.	Reduce feed when leaves change, but keep feeding evergreens.	Stop feeding deciduous trees, but give evergreens one more application in late fall.

Glossary of Feeding Terms

High nitrogen. Most plant nurseries sell a selection of regular plant foods. These have a high-nitrogen mix, such as N-18 P-12 K-12. This is the breakdown of the macro-nutrients called nitrogen, phosphorus, and potassium. As long as the nitrogen content is slightly higher than the other nutrients, this will be fine. Brand names vary around the world, so visit your local garden center and get a regular house-plant food if that is all that is available. High nitrogen is used to force green growth. Most of these feeds will have essential trace elements included. Do not use lawn or grass food, as they are far too high in nitrogen for a bonsai.

Low nitrogen. This is when the phosphorus and the potassium levels are higher than the nitrogen content. Again, brands will vary according to where in the world you live. Low nitrogen content is used to stop the growth of leaves and needles during the early spring and fall, and is designed to feed the bark and roots instead.

Balanced feed. This is when the feed contains about equal-level N.P.K.

Specialist feed. There are many specialist feeds designed for plants such as lime-hating plants, heathers, and azaleas.

Cake feeds. These are placed on top of the soil, into which they will slowly release nutrients. They are a better method for feeding established trees. Pellet feeds are slow-release feeds that are placed into the soil at repotting time. They have limited usefulness, as you are unable to control the feed action should something go wrong. On the other hand, using them in the garden when planting out can be advantageous.

Pests and Diseases

Each country has its fair share of little pests trying to survive. On a general note, we all hate these little devils; an attack of black aphid can destroy a healthy tree in a couple of days. The insidiousness of vine weevil can destroy many trees by the time you realize that they have been attacked. This section looks at common pests, and provides ways in which to reduce their presence. These pests can rarely be eradicated completely.

SCALE INSECT

This pest looks like a small lump on the trunk or branch and can be rubbed off with your finger. Usually light- to dark-brown in color, the scale can mimic the natural color of the bark. Be diligent, as scale insects are sap-suckers. Most bonsai can be attacked by scale insects, but be especially watchful if you keep elms or zelkovas, although over seventy species of trees have been noted as being susceptible to them. Use a systemic insecticide to control them, as tiny ones can be missed in the cracks in the bark.

RIGHT A scale insect, revealing the weblike mass around its carapace.

RIGHT A scale insect with its eggs.

FAR RIGHT Black fly – an aphid.

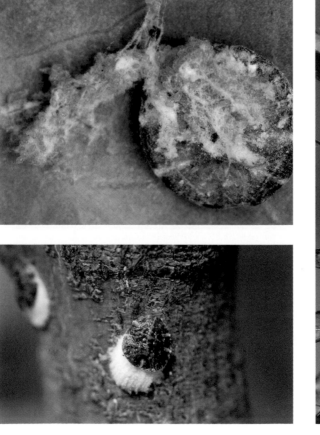

BELOW Adelgids.

APHID: ROOT APHID, GREEN, WHITE, AND BLACK APHID

Another sap-sucker that can affect most species of tree, there are many varieties of aphids, and because they multiply at a huge rate they must be dealt with quickly. The bane of rose and fruit growers, aphids can be killed by application of insecticide specific to them. They can carry secondary diseases, such as leaf wilt, and cause sooty mold after leaving their detritus on leaves and branches. In my own observation, it appears that green aphids will attack young buds and leaves, while black aphids will attack branches and twigs. The black aphid is more destructive than the green, again from my own experience, and can transfer disease from one plant to another. Be diligent and rub off as many as you can with your fingers, or spray them with an insecticide, such as malathion, three times during the first week of infestation. Apply the insecticide

RIGHT Leaf-miner
damage.

RIGHT Leaf-miner
damage.

RIGHT Bark-miner
damage on a tree trunk.

They look like balls of cotton wool in the base of pine or larch needles. On pines, you need to hose as many as possible off, making sure that you do not move them on to other trees. Spray the tree at least three times during the first week, then wash off the wooly remains and reapply the insecticide once a week for three weeks. Wooly aphids are more common on pines and larches.

LEAF MINER

Leaf miners are the larvae of leaf flies. The larvae burrow into the leaf from an egg that has been laid on its underside. Long threads of discoloration appear, which are their tunnels. Treat the tree with a systemic and remove affected leaves. New leaves will then reappear.

BARK MINER

Examples of bark miners are Dutch elm beetle and bark weevils. They can devastate a plant slowly, and without your knowledge. Keep a

with your normal misting spray. It is also a good idea to spray any other trees around your bonsai as well. The key times for spraying are spring and fall, but keep spraying, as they are persistent.

ADELGID AND WOOLY APHID

Adelgids and wooly aphids are also sap-suckers.

close eye out during the year for little holes, sometimes with sawdust coming out of them – like woodworm – or discolored bark areas. The worst victims are large bonsai, as they are so big that damage could have been inflicted for a couple of years before things get really out of hand. Once identified, treat with a systemic every week for two months. If large or small areas of bark are dead, you will have to remove them to get at the grubs, as well as the adults. At worst, you will have a dead tree, and at the best you will have a beetle-induced Shari. Long-horned Formosan beetles are wood-borers and sometimes come with imported bonsai or trees. They are very big and very hungry. These beetles are black, with white spots and long antennae.

RIGHT A vine-weevil grub discovered while repotting.

ABOVE The adult weevil. Weevils are pests everywhere, so your weevil could be of a different variety to the one shown here. The vine weevil was originally known as a pest that attacked vines in vineyards. (It has always attacked any plant, but it was most noticeable in vineyards.) If it attacks your bonsai or garden plants, you must eradicate it. Keep a vigilant eye open, as it could have come into your garden from a neighboring one.

VINE WEEVILS
Vine weevils are hard to identify, as the larvae can stay in the soil for six months, eating roots, and it may only be at the repotting stage that you find them. Adult insects eat the leaves around the edges. There are special proprietary solutions to handle them, and these are available from bonsai suppliers or nurseries. They are usually based on either Nematodes or Gamma HCH.

RED SPIDER MITES
Red spider mites are not always red, but look like dust if you shake a bit of foliage on to your hand. Red spider mites attack many plants, but needle-juniper varieties are especially susceptible to them. Spraying and systemic will sort them out over a period of three or four weeks.

ABOVE A froghopper building its bubble nest.

RIGHT Mildew – fungal growth on leaves.

BELOW A minigroup of olives (*Olea*). Olives are particularly popular in Europe and South Africa because of their vigor.

FROGHOPPERS

Commonly known as "cuckoo spit," the froghopper is a jumping insect that lives in a nest of bubbles. When you push your finger into the bubbles, you expose a pale-green insect that will invariably jump away like a minigrasshopper. It feeds on the plant's sap. Removal is by systemic, because if it is disturbed it will simply hop away – usually on to another plant.

LEATHERJACKETS

Cranefly larvae, or root-cutters, are sometimes known as leather-jackets, as they have a hard, dark-brown or black casing to their pupae. They are dark-gray or brown and like a caterpillar or mealworm, depending on the species. They eat living roots and cut them in any direction. Root-cutters can also be beetle larvae, such as weevils.

MILDEW

Mildew is formed when plants are not getting sufficient air circulation and in areas of high humidity. Use a specialist fungicide to treat mildew, such as rose mildew treatments.

DO NOT ALLOW THE FUNGICIDE TO PENETRATE THE SOIL
Protect the soil with a cloth and polythene. The fungicide may damage beneficial cultures growing in the bonsai soil.

Troubleshooting

If you follow the correct watering and feeding regimes, your bonsai should thrive, but problems can occur if you are a beginner. Most are preventable or curable, as long as they are caught in time. Unfortunately, it is all too common for a tree to have died before the owner has noticed that there is something wrong, so it always pays to be diligent. If you spend only one minute a day with each of your bonsai, closely studying it for malfunction, pests, and anything else, you will always stay ahead of trouble. This section looks at common problems, and how to treat them.

Dehydration

Dehydration is indicated by dry soil, yellowing and falling leaves, as well as little wrinkles on the trunk and branches. (This wrinkling can also indicate overwatering, when the bonsai is unable to take in any more water and the roots have rotted. This problem is covered later.)

SOLUTION: It may be too late, but water the tree and, of course, let it drain. The tree may not take up water if the soil has dried out. If this is the case, then put the tree in a basin and immerse the soil in it for ten minutes. If the water is being taken up by the soil – indicated by the soil sending up air bubbles – let it drain and then put it in a large, clear, polythene bag. Spray it with a fungicide to prevent botrytis (powdery mildew). Close the top of the bag and allow the humidity to build up. Keep the tree at normal temperature, or, in a hot climate, in the shade. This may force the growth to work through the system. Check after two weeks and open the top of the bag.

Overwatering

Overwatering is indicated by wet soil, slime mold, or algae on the surface of the soil. This is usually dark green and slimy to the touch.

SOLUTION: First make sure that you have some sterile, fine, plant grit, Akadama soil, or baked-clay granules used for horticulture. Small-sized hydroponics grit or Perlag is fine. The soil needs to drain quickly so that the medium can quickly dry out to avoid permanently damp soil. Lift the tree from the pot and carefully remove the soil. Gently wash off the soil with a fine spray, exposing all of the roots. Check to see if any of them are dead, bark is peeling off them, for wet wood, slime mold and, of course, larvae, such as leatherjackets or other root-cutting insects. Cut off the dead roots and, on large trees, seal them with a wound-sealant for trees (Lac balsam, Kiyonal, tree-wound paint etc.). Dust the roots lightly with rooting hormone powder and plant in the new mix. Spray the tree with a fungicide and put it into a large polythene bag and seal it. Make a few holes underneath the bag to allow the drainage of excess water. Ensure that the soil is lightly watered and drained, if required. Keep the tree in the bag for two weeks and then open it at the top. Leave it for a further two weeks

LEFT A small fig (*Ficus*). This is good material for bonsai in warm climates.

before lifting out the tree. Growth should have started. This solution is not the panacea to all ills. If your tree is too damaged, it will not recover.

LEFT A Chinese juniper (*Juniperus chinensis*). This species responds well to the plucking out of new growth.

RIGHT A minihornbeam (*Carpinus*). Miniature bonsai are more difficult to keep than larger styles. Smaller trees need more care because they have less soil.

The Tree is Not Clearing Water From the Soil Surface

This can be an indication that the tree needs repotting. It can also mean that something is affecting the soil, such as leatherjackets or other pests. It is also an indication that the soil is compacted or incorrect.

SOLUTION 1: If the tree needs repotting, do it immediately. Most trees can be repotted at any time of the year if it is an emergency. The trick is not to remove all of the soil, but to leave 80 percent. Do not disturb the roots and plant it in a bigger container until the correct potting season.

SOLUTION 2: Soak the tree's soil in a basin to try to get water into the roots. If there are cranefly or other leatherjacket-type larvae, then some will emerge immediately. If they do, drop some insecticide into the solution to force the rest out.

SOLUTION 3: If the soil is compacted and you know that the tree was recently repotted, lift it out of the pot and rake away some of the outside and surface soil. Rake underneath the soil mass.

Carefully insert a chopstick and wriggle it around slightly, first one way and then the other, to open out the soil. Work right through the soil mass. Replace the soil around the outside and underneath the tree with small grit, between 2 and 3mm (⅒"), to increase the drainage. If your chopstick holes are big, then drop some grit into the holes as well. If the tree is a new purchase, you may find that it has a clay-type soil under a surface of normal potting soil. It is difficult for the beginner to attempt a complete soil change, so it is best just to make sure that the soil does not dry out until repotting can be safely done. At that point you will have to leave at least 50 percent of the clay soil and tease out the roots around the outside. These may be brittle, so be careful. Using a normal potting mix (see the section on soils), carefully arrange the roots in the new soil, but do not cut any of them unless they are dead. This may apply to indoor trees that come from China, where they tend to use a dense clay for soil. It is acceptable as a medium for some Chinese trees, but in other climates the humidity levels can be dry. This makes the clay harden, which dries out the root system, causing the tree to die. In the U.K. this soil is removed by order of the Department of Agriculture as it can harbor pests.

BELOW Care and attention will keep bonsai healthy in colder months. This is an elm (*Ulmus*) in winter. It is 1m (40") tall.

YOUR PINE OR JUNIPER HAS STARTED TO TURN BROWN

This can happen at any time, and usually your options are few. It can indicate a number of things, including an insect attack, overwatering, or dehydration. There are some techniques that can be tried if all else fails. Note that *Cryptomeria*, yew (*Taxus*), box (*Buxus*), cypress (*Chamaecyparis*), and many more evergreens, *except* for pines, naturally display a glossy, brown tinge during the winter or cold months in temperate climates.

SOLUTION: Soak some long sphagnum moss in a B1-vitamin solution (two crushed pills in a cup of water). Brand-name solutions can also be used. Remove the tree from the pot and tease out the roots. Leave the center section of soil on the root ball and wrap the moss around the root mass. Place the root ball in a deep, plastic, plant pot to cover the moss. Cut off the obviously dead roots and seal the cuts. Wrap the entire pot, moss and all, in a plastic bag and spray the upper portion three times a day with the vitamin solution. Make sure that the top of the tree does not stay wet – just mist it.

In low-humidity or dehydration situations, enclose the entire unit in a plastic bag for two weeks, but keep an eye on the tree. Leave the top of the bag open to allow air circulation. Evergreens do not like turgid air, and this high humidity can sometimes be too much for them.

ABOVE These are miniature white pines grafted onto normal black pine stock (base trunks). They are 11cm (4½") high.

LEFT Unlike pine or juniper, it is normal for the foliage of *Cryptomeria* to turn brown in winter.

Keeping Your Bonsai in Shape

One way to find good surface-root shape on nursery stock is to see if the tree has a number of low-growing branches. These will reflect a good nebari or surface roots. Nursery stock with the first branch higher up on the trunk can indicate a one-sided root formation – not a pleasant image. The artistic value of a tree with plenty of fine twigs, buds, branches, and roots advertises your ability as a bonsai-grower or, in slightly less grand terms, as a grower of miniature trees.

BELOW Wide nebari is a feature of maples (*Acers*), and elms (*Ulmus*).

BELOW RIGHT The nebari of these trees are similar to the nebari of Chinese elms.

Pruning, Pinching and Plucking

The reason why you should prune and pluck is to develop the dense twig structure that creates the miniature image of a full-sized tree. The more that you understand plucking (or pinching), the better your bonsai will look.

Building the Branch Structure

One of the most important lessons in developing bonsai involves the branch-and-twig structure (ramification). The health of the tree depends on your ability to create more and more twigs, as these produce the leaves that allow the tree to breathe. The physiological advantages of more twigs and branches are that increasingly fine root development takes place, giving the tree a solid base to stand on. Roots also help to define twigs. A tree root mirrors the branch shape, although it is generally more compacted. This is another reason for trimming the roots: to keep the bonsai in a pot and also to encourage secondary growth on the roots, which will in turn encourage secondary twigs on the branch structure.

LEFT To understand what is meant by nebari, you need to see what surface-root structure is all about. Nebari is a Japanese word meaning "surface root," and it is the most difficult aspect of bonsai creation. This redwood trunk shows how a well-shaped tree swells out at the base.

ABOVE The very large base of this old oak is unusual, but still constitutes an interesting nebari.

RIGHT Forest groups of bonsai often lack good nebari, but, as you can see, this is not always true in real forests.

ABOVE A short swelling is also good nebari.

ABOVE Zelkova, identified by the red stem of the new growth. This shows the length of stem that needs to be cut back. Cut back to the first set of new leaves on the top and upper third of the bonsai. Cut back to the second set on the next third, and to the third set on the last third. This will eventually start to build fine twigs in a treelike shape. Wiring and pruning form the structure, but definition can be achieved by pruning. These bonsai techniques should be performed during the growing season.

ABOVE RIGHT Similar new growth on a birch (*Betula*). Cut back most deciduous varieties in the same way.

Pruning

ELMS, ZELKOVAS, PRIVETS, AND HEMLOCK

In general, pruning back to the first set of buds at the top of the tree and to the second set at the side of the tree will force new growth in those areas. You are trying to create a tree shape, so you must start with an outline. This cutting-back technique then continues three or so times a year – always allowing the tree to grow in between – cutting back to the first set of new buds on the top and the second set at the sides. As the tree grows and flourishes, you can cut back to the third set of new buds at the lower sides of the tree to create a domed shape reminiscent of a mature tree. To keep the shape, you will have to continue to prune in this manner every year.

Pinching

JUNIPERUS, CRYPTOMERIA, AND OTHER SCALE-TYPE LEAVES

With scale-type leaves, hold the cluster of needles or foliage firmly, and, without twisting the tip, pluck out the new growth at the tips. Repeat at least three times throughout the spring and late summer. This will encourage the foliage to thicken up on these branches. The trouble with junipers is that the growth will continue to the end of the branch if you do not do this, when you will have long, spindly branches with a ball of foliage at the end. Pinching will encourage the foliage to stay within the structure of the tree. To keep the shape, you will have to continue to prune in this manner every year. You will also have to cut out some foliage every two or three years because it will become very dense.

RIGHT Pinching out new growth on a scale-foliage tree, such as *Juniperus chinensis* and *Chamaecyparis obtusa*.

BELOW Plucking out new growth on juniper-needle foliage, such as *Juniperus squamata, communis,* and *rigida.* Just pluck out the new tips to create dense foliage pads.

Pruning and Plucking-out

MAPLES

This technique develops new buds, which will form where the bonsai has been injured. Many species do this. The only problem that you will then have is developing the new growth from these points. It will take about five years to achieve a new shape. Interestingly, you can also leave length on a branch to increase the outline should it fall short of the overall design plan.

The correct way in which to get dense growth on maples is to pluck out the new growth at the center of the bud when the tree opens in spring. This will encourage the tree to develop finer, denser growth on its second spurt. However, with a young tree you can also cut back the branches in summer, when it is too hot to grow leaves and the tree is in its mid-season period of dormancy. If the tree is vigorous, it will then develop new buds all over the branch. Every time you cut one branch tip, two new ones will grow.

Another species that you must pluck out when new growth appears is beech. Wait until the pointed bud swells and half unfurls, then pluck out the center. The secondary leaves will be smaller and the tree will become denser.

LEFT On this snake bark maple (*Acer davidii*) you can see new buds developing near the stem of the branch and at the base of one of the existing leaves.

LEFT A huge branch has been pruned from this maple. After four years, the wound has almost healed. You can see an example of wire marks damaging the fine bark of the new branches of a tree.

Leaf-cutting For Finer Twigs and Leaves

Leaf-cutting can be carried out on most deciduous species, both indoor and outdoor. It is best to do this once a year to young, or extremely vigorous, trees, but only every two or three years to more established bonsai. Some climates have the kind of weather that allows defoliation three times in one year, but do not do this more than once in a temperate climate. Do not feed the tree when defoliating it and keep the soil damp.

With maples, you should cut off nearly all of the leaves, just under the part where the leaf joins the thin stem that attaches it to the branch. This is called the petiole, and leaving it on will help a new bud to develop at the base of each leaf stem. Leave one or two leaves at the end of each branch to force the sap to move to the outer part of the branch, but remove all of the rest. The second set of leaves will appear within three or four weeks. The effect will be to increase the density of the leaves while making them smaller and in better proportion.

Stem-cutting Deciduous Trees

When stem-cutting deciduous trees, either cut just below a set of leaves to get vigorous growth or, as the illustration shows, just above a set of leaves for smaller growth. With most bonsai, it is best to develop the tree to a plan. You need

Case Study: Developing New Buds

▲ 1 Here you can see overall growth in late spring.

▶ 2 With sharp scissors, cut back to the first set of leaves on the new growth. Also remove any leaves that are larger than normal throughout the growing season.

◀ 3 To achieve smaller leaves and denser growth on maples, look for the new growth during the spring. This also keeps the internodes (the distance between the leaves) short.

▲ 4 Carefully pluck out the center of this new growth.

either a drawing or a photograph of how your tree should look. As a rough guide, starting at the top of the tree, cut back to the second set of leaves – that is, leaving two pairs of leaves at that point – and to the third set at the sides. What then happens is that the cut areas force the tree to grow new buds below the cut at the base of the remaining last set of leaves. When they grow five or six sets of leaves, cut them back in the same way, until you build up a structure.

Pruning Indoor Bonsai

When removing leaves, it is also a good time to shape the bare branches. Leave 10 percent of the leaves on indoor trees when defoliating. The new

buds will start to appear within three weeks. In between, keep the soil damp and do not feed. This technique can be used for most indoor trees.

Branch-pruning

You need to branch-prune when branches are crossing each other and cannot be wired out. It can also be done to reduce the length of a branch, to get rid of an opposing branch (a bar branch), or to remove a very thick or very thin branch that is out of proportion with the rest of the tree's structure. In some cases, you can even remove all of the branches and start again.

Seal all cuts after pruning as this will stop the tips of the new cuts from dying back

ABOVE To prune mature or hardened maple leaves, cut back to the first set of leaves. Cut just short of the last set if the tree is healthy, or just under the second-last set if the tree is slow in vigor.

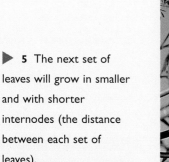

▶ **5** The next set of leaves will grow in smaller and with shorter internodes (the distance between each set of leaves).

◀ **6** Leaving a long shoot will not thicken a tree – for that, you need to cut back the long shoot by half, grow side shoots, and repeat the procedure until a branch has developed. After it has thickened up the area you want, the temporary branch can be cut off. This technique develops an apex, or top, to a tree, especially in maples.

▲ **7** By the end of spring, this maple has become overgrown. You can see the primary shape and where the excess length should be trimmed back to recover the design. It is better to prune it lightly throughout spring to prevent this.

Case Study: Branch-pruning

SUBJECT: CHINESE ELM

Ulmus parvifolia (Ulmus sinensis/Ulmus seiboldii)
Chinese elm is both an indoor and outdoor species and is rarely affected by disease. It needs watering and hates bad frost, but is otherwise one of the easiest of all of the bonsai subjects. The tree featured here was recently imported and has had little shaping. The root nebari, or surface-root appearance, is not too bad, although it has a number of faults, such as crossing roots and an imbalance of root height on one side. This can be corrected by shaping and dropping the tree deeper into the pot.

The overall foliage mass will not take much work to make it a nice bonsai or penjing. It has a small branch that sticks out and disturbs the balance of the tree (in my opinion, of course). In penjing that feature would be used to good effect, but I decided that the tree was going to become a bonsai instead and that the branch structure would be more rigorously defined.

To make the tree look bigger, I decided to cut off the branch and seal the cut with Cut paste. Some countries have their own brand of tree-wound putty, and, at worst, grafting wax will do. Cut paste is better, however. You could import it using the Internet, but note that importing it into some countries can be problematical, as the Japanese packaging makes it difficult to identify.

◀ **3** Using another type of concave cutter, called a wen or knob-cutter, the flat area is cut into, making a slightly hollow cut.

▼ **4** The hollowed-out cut took just one cut from the wen cutter to make. This will allow the bark to grow over and the cut section eventually to disappear, within four years on this size of tree.

▲ **1** The tree before removing the smaller, thinner branch.

▶ **2** Using an angled cutter, the lower branch is removed right back to the trunk without touching the trunk's bark.

▲ **5** Make a hollow in the Cut paste or tree putty with your thumb.

▶ **6** Fill the hollow with water, which allows you to handle the paste without it sticking to your fingers. The paste will still stick to the tree and can be smoothed over easily.

▼ **7** Take a small piece of paste and roll it into a ball.

◀ **8** Apply the ball to the center of the cut. On larger cuts, roll the paste into a tube and apply it around the edges of the cut and seal the center with Lac Balsam, Kiyonal, or your own bonsai wound-sealer.

◀ **9** Smooth over the paste, using a little more water if required, and leave it until it falls off of its own accord. On pines and heavy-barked trees, you can even stick some bark to the Cut paste and disguise the cut completely.

▼ **10** The resulting, better-balanced image. The two foliage pads will be pruned and wired into two soft triangles, making a bigger overall triangle.

ABOVE Natural jinn (dead branches) and shari (dead areas of trunk) on this pine (*Pinus*).

Creating Shari
● Only employ this technique on a well-established tree and not on a recently repotted bonsai.
● Unless you are very experienced, never take off more than one-third of the width of the tree.
● Draw the shape that you wish to cut out on the tree with a pencil or fine marker pen.
● Using a very sharp knife, cut through the bark until you reach the wood. Do this on all sides of the shape.
● Slide the knife carefully under the bark and lift it off. The bark should be easy to remove.
● Seal all cut edges with a latex wound-sealer.
● Treat with a watered-down solution of fungicide – not lime-sulfur solution at this stage. It is fine to treat the jinn with lime sulfur, as long as you have used a latex-based wound-sealant or putty to seal the base of the jinn where it meets the trunk, or where you have left the bark on.

When removing crossing roots on the surface, or where there are nebari or surface roots, do it in such a way as to disguise the cut if possible. Another alternative to cutting a crossing root is to rewire the root into a new position, but note that surface roots are prone to cracking, so wrap the root in raffia before wiring and shaping it (see the repotting section).

Special Age Effects: Jinn and Shari

Making jinn and shari are some of the ways in which to age a bonsai. Jinn is a method of cutting a branch that is extra to the design. Cutting the branch short, carefully cut around the bark at the base of the branch and remove the bark from the stump. Either carve the jinned area into a natural point or split the end and pull it down, without extending it, on to the trunk. This looks like a broken branch in nature. Seal the bottom of the jinn where it meets the tree with a latex-based tree-wound-sealer – normally available from a bonsai nursery or seller. Brand names include Lac Balsam, Kiyonal, and (my preference), Cut paste.

To whiten or gray the jinn, use lime-sulfur or jinn solution. Lime-sulfur solution turns the bark white, while mixing it with a little sumi ink or black watercolor ink produces a light-gray color

Root-pruning

Pruning a third of the outer roots during each repotting will encourage new roots. Removing major subsurface roots can also be done, but remember to seal the bigger cuts in case they rot. When I cut a big root, I always dust it lightly with rooting hormone powder.

after the jinn or shari has dried. Treatment should take place in late spring, and making three applications during the first year is normal practice. Each year, wash off any remaining old solution and reapply in sunny, dry weather. Lime sulfur preserves the dead wood. It is better to use some wood preservative on the larger dead areas, too, as these will rot if they are in the soil. Make sure that you do not touch any of the living tissue, however. Never allow lime sulfur to get into the roots, as it is a fungicide and will destroy the beneficial mycelium fungus that lives in symbiosis with the tree.

You would usually have one or two trunk jinns, but on tall, slim trees, or groups of tall trees, there could be many more. These emulate the stumps of dead branches in forest trees, which are caused when the tree's top branches reach for the light, while the lower areas are shaded, causing the lower branches to die.

Shari used to be called sharimiki, which means "stickleback" or "fish bones." The technique was to cut away a section of bark that only had a few branches. This exposed the wood underneath the bark and, after trimming and carving the jinns, would give the tree an aged appearance. The technique grew into encompassing the removal of any trunk bark, a slightly more advanced technique.

ABOVE To make a jinn, you need to cut away the bark in most cases (certain jinns require some bark to be left on as part of the design).

RIGHT In this example, the yew (*Taxus*), has a shari all the way up the trunk. This is emphasized by incorporating natural jinns three-quarters of the way up.

ABOVE In this case we are working on a collected hawthorn (*Crataegus*). The top was too high, so we needed to do something with the stump.

ABOVE Carving the entire structure with a router (an electric wood-carving tool) moves the wood quickly and gives a nice result, which is incorporated into the design. The jinn in this area is supposed to emulate a lightening-struck tree that has rotted a little.

RIGHT Lac Balsam and Kiyonal are popular wound-sealers. Brand names may change in different countries, but these brands are sold in both North America and Europe.

ABOVE Jinning pliers are used to remove bark or twist wire; also pictured here are wire and wire-cutters.

LEFT Natural jinn and shari are emulated in this *Juniperus chinensis sargentii*.

RIGHT On this *Juniperus chinensis sargentii* the jinn is part of the design.

ABOVE Examples of natural jinn on a pine.

RIGHT Here is a larch (*Larix*) that needs some refinement. Instead of removing the branches completely, it was decided to jinn them.

FAR RIGHT Turning the tree around, we jinned the excess branches and wired the tree into a better shape, using the jinns as part of the design.

What is Wiring?

Wiring is the principal method used for shaping bonsai. For many years copper wire was the most popular kind of wire, but it has since been replaced with aluminum, which is easier to bend. Aluminum wire is either silver colored or, preferably, copper anodized. It comes in around ten thicknesses, from 1 to 6mm, including ½mm.

Copper is still used by some growers, but unless it is annealed – softened by heat – it is impossible to bend thicker wires. Once it is bent, the molecular structure hardens again and small alterations on anything but the thinnest of copper wire can be difficult. Copper wire does, however, have a place when bending the branches of species, like cedars, that have a tendency to be springy and that may revert to shape.

Wire should not be unwound from the bonsai for reuse, as unwinding it may damage the buds, bark, and twigs. All wire must instead be cut off the tree. Because it is harder, copper wire is less thick than aluminum wire.

Reasons For Wiring

- To bend a branch, twigs, or even roots.
- To straighten branches.
- To shape the overall appearance of the bonsai.
- To reshape a single branch, apex of the bonsai, and so on.

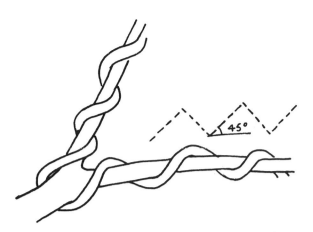

ABOVE Single wiring.

support the branches. As you can see from the diagram, the wire is put on at a 45° angle. When you reach another branch, reverse the direction of the wire by going around the trunk or supporting branch and bringing the wire up in the opposite direction. All wire must be anchored well into a joint, as shown. Reversing the direction one way at the branch joint will enable you to anchor the wire correctly.

When to Wire

The best time to wire many species of bonsai is in late winter. In temperate climates, you can also wire in mid-summer, when the tree is in its mid-season dormancy period. In humid climates, it is best to wire in late winter, in early spring, before bud break, and in late fall.

Single Wiring

Single wiring is the mainstay of bonsai-shaping and is used on small areas. It is important that you understand the reverse direction needed to

Multiple Wiring

Multiple wiring simply entails increasing the number of wires to enable faster wiring and subsequently spurring off on to smaller twigs.

I started using this technique with beginners, as it made it both easier to understand wiring and harder to make mistakes, such as wires crossing over on each other. If all of the wires are going the same way, it makes for much neater wiring

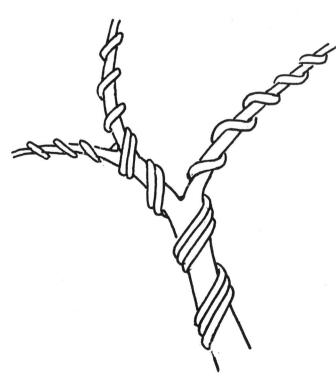

ABOVE Multiple wiring.

Case Study: Juniper NURSERY-MATERIAL TRANSFORMATION

▲ **1** I was teaching at a workshop in Wales when my host brought in this large *Juniperus squamata*. It took about four hours to wire.

▼ **2** After I had shaped it, a much more treelike image had developed. Excellent wiring had helped me to find the image.

Case Study: Designing a Large Yew *(Taxus)* – GARDEN CENTER MATERIAL

▲ **1** This is a large, nursery yew that I worked on over the course of a workshop in Belgium. The tops of the branches have been cut and the clump left for a year. It is in an extremely small pot.

▶ **2** Too many trunks meant that one should either come out or, as we decided, be completely jinned. We also removed a large crossing root at the front. Although I wanted to develop only one side of the tree and jinn the rest, I knew that it would stress the plant. I needed a healthy tree to work on in four years' time.

▲ **3** The wiring took three people about three hours. You can see the spot from which the root was removed. If you look closely, you can also see a bit of carving that I did to reduce the stump in that area.

▼ **5** The completed tree. I wanted to remove either the left or the right side, as the removal of either would have made a nice tree. The owner decided that he would follow my plan and would grow it on both sides to begin with to make the tree healthy again. The upper portion is very vigorous, but the roots need to develop a lot more to give real strength. It will take about three years of pinching to establish a softer shape and for the foliage pads to soften out. You can see how the wiring gives the tree shape. Three years later the tree is very healthy and is developing into the required design.

▲ **4** After shaping the branches into the final image, we then repotted the tree into a larger container. What little there was of the existing root ball was teased out as much as possible to give the roots a good start in their new pot.

Case Study: Advanced Wiring - Spruce (*PICEA ABIES*)

▲ **1** This spruce was collected in the Italian Alps. It is a good example of wiring a tree into a bonsai shape. It will take a lot of work to pluck and develop the growth, but the skeletal structure has now been organized.

◀ **3** The thin, soft twigs have been styled into the tree's body shape. These must now thicken. After the tips have been plucked, and with correct feeding, the tree will develop body.

▼ **4** The apex, or top, of the tree has also been designed using thinner material. There is no other way in which to achieve such a tree shape.

▲ **2** These large branches were removed, but short stubs were left and were in turn jinned.

throughout. All wiring techniques must have one thing in common, however: the wire must be firmly anchored so that it doesn't slip, otherwise the branch will not stay in the required shape. Always keep an even distance between the coils of wires.

In the diagrams you can see that I use three wires. When the wires reach a new branch I spur off on to it with one wire. When I reach another branch I repeat the procedure until all of the wires have been used up. I use a variety of different wire sizes to match the branch size.

Remove the wires from the vigorous part of the tree if the tree grows rapidly and the wire starts to bite into the branch.

Multiple Wiring From the Trunk Into the Branches

To take multiple wiring from the trunk into the branches, first carefully push the wires into the soil, to avoid damaging the roots. Then carefully

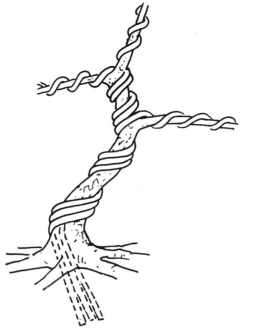

LEFT Multiple wiring from the trunk into the branches.

wind the wire up the trunk at a 45° angle, spurring off into the branches. Trunks can be bent, too, and normally straight, featureless trunks can be shaped to make them more attractive.

Case Study: Scots Pine (*PINUS SYLVESTRIS*) – WORKSHOP WIRING TRANSFORMATION

▲ **1** I was teaching at a workshop in Southampton, England, when this leggy pine arrived. It was very tall – over 1m (40') – but did not have much in the way of branches.

▼ **2** After the owner had wired up the trunk and branches, I styled the tree into a literati, or mountain-image, pine.

▲ **3** I am careful to make sure that all of the trees that I design are equally attractive on all sides. There should always be a front to a tree, as well as a back and two sides. Each of these elements should look as good as the others.

Case Study: Workshop Transformation — *CHAMAECYPARIS*

▼ **2** A couple of hours later Simon had completed the wiring and I could then start to help him to restore the bonsai image.

▲ **1** I worked on this tree with Simon Misdale, a student of Robert Langholm, New Zealand's most experienced bonsai master. Simon wanted to refine this *Chamaecyparis*, which had grown out of shape. I decided that it needed a full rewire, so we cleaned off the lichens and started wiring. It is always a good idea to mist any tree that you are wiring, as stress-induced transpiration can damage it.

Cage Wiring

Cage wiring prevents wire marks from developing on young, fast-growing shoots as you use a slightly thicker wire than the branch would normally need. Making sure that the wire does not squeeze the branch, wind it around the branch into the required shape (one side may just touch the branch). This forms a cage for the branch to grow through. It is less stressful on the branch than other forms of wiring and is particularly useful when training young shoots on maples and many other species. It is very good for winter wiring, as it will not bite into spring growth as quickly.

LEFT Cage wiring is a technique that I developed over a number of years to reduce damage caused to fine branches.

Case Study: Styling From Nursery Stock— LARCH (*LARIX*)

◀ **3** Next we went to work on the wiring.

▼ **4** After two hours Robert had created this fine image of a tree. That is the beauty of wiring.

▲ **1** Robert Porch has been working with me for a number of years now, and we were running workshops in Belgium when this very tall larch arrived for a demonstration of wiring.

▶ **2** Robert first identified the root nebari and then chose the optimum viewing angle, based on the best root image.

Potting and Repotting a Bonsai

Potting a bonsai, or repotting a tree that has outgrown its pot, can be daunting tasks for the beginner. Soil type is an important consideration, and depends on the variety of tree that you have, but providing the correct balance of ingredients is the key. It is also vital that your bonsai is in a suitable pot, one that will allow the roots room to grow, but that will also complement the appearance of your tree.

Soils

The bonsai soil should be free-draining at all times. I will not discuss every kind of soil that is available, but will instead give you an idea of what to look for for an ideal bonsai-planting soil. Conifers prefer a dryer soil, so a higher proportion of grit, which allows more drainage, is better for these, while flowering trees prefer a higher organic content to the soil. Indoor trees may need a higher proportion of organic matter as well. Repot using dry mix, not wet mixed soil.

Ingredients of Bonsai Soil

GRIT: Fine grit can be 1 to 2mm and should be sharp. Local grit is available around the world, and is sometimes known as river sand. However, inhaling granite grit dust is carcinogenic, so always take precautions before using it.. Pile it outside the house and hose it down at once. Take enough wet grit for your soil mix, put it in a sieve, and hose the grit through it. It is now safe to use. Do not use builder's sand, which is either too fine or contains too much lime.

BELOW A selection of antique pots on display.

ORGANIC MATTER: This can be leaf mold, fine, composted bark, or peat. When using leaf mold, you must make sure that it is sterile. Otherwise the insects and fungus that may be in the leaves could be transferred to your soil mix. If you have a microwave, put some leaf mold in a plastic bowl and blast it for five minutes. Do not use garden soil or loam, which has an unknown constitution and can cause problems with root formation. I advocate the use of peat-based organic material. The only thing that you must remember when using peat is that if it dries out you will be unable to rehydrate it, which could cause problems, so make sure that your watering regime is correct.

Water-retentive, but also noncompactive, materials include Akadama (red soil), Kanuma-Azalea (yellow soil or red-clay granules), Biosorb, and some proprietary names that originate in Japan. There are some excellent American brands as well. These soil materials are available from most local bonsai suppliers, but if you can't find any use a mix of organic matter and grit instead. Nowadays, Akadama is used in many countries around the world. Note that there are different qualities of Japanese soil and different particle sizes of granules. They are generally identified by either the standard grade or the superior, double-red-line grade. There are other levels of quality available, too.

Soil-formula Mixes

YOUNG CONIFERS
Pure Akadama can be used with pines and other conifers, but I prefer to add a percentage of grit and peat to the mix for balance. For an organic element, retain some nutrients when applying. A good conifer mix is 60 percent Akadama, 20 percent grit, and 20 percent peat.

ESTABLISHED CONIFERS
The soil should consist of 60 percent grit and 40 percent organic. Older-established specimen conifers can use a 70 percent grit and 30 percent organic mix.

LIME-HATING ERICACEOUS SPECIES
Azaleas and rhododendrons like lime-free soils, so a ratio of 70 percent organic to 30 percent grit gives good water retention, soft soil, and adequate drainage. Specialist soils from Japan are designed for specific kinds of lime-hating bonsai.

DECIDUOUS (NONERICACEOUS)
Use a 60 percent organic and 40 percent grit mix.

INDOOR SPECIES
Indoor bonsai require differing soil depending on species, for example, figs like 80 to 90 percent organic and the balance in grit, while *sageritia* and *serissa* like 70 percent organic and 30 percent grit.

Proportions are measured using same size of measuring cups, handfuls, or spades, depending on the amount of repotting that you are planning.

Always prepare your soils a few days prior to the potting day.

Whatever type of soil mix you use is fine, as long as the combination roughly follows the above guidelines. Your local nursery or bonsai club will advise you. Soil-mixing can be one of the most intimidating areas of bonsai culture for beginners, but do not let it put you off. The truth is that as long as the tree has some kind of quick-draining soil it will nearly always survive, no matter what the soil is composed of. It is the correct proportions of that growing medium that will determine the optimum health of the tree.

LEFT Any good bonsai nursery will have a wide selection of pots in all sizes.

Case Study: A Bonsai That Needs a Bigger Pot

▼ **4** The root ball is still very dry, as there is little soil, but there are enough fine roots for development.

▲ **5** A much bigger pot is used, to allow the roots to spread out.

▼ **6** Following the basic potting technique, the tree is placed on a mound of soil and the potting procedure is then gradually finished.

▲ **I** This bonsai has not been repotted for four years, which is two years too long for such a shallow pot.

▶ **2** When the tree has been taken out of the pot, the roots are very dense. All of the nutrients were used up long ago and there is little, if any, soil left in the pot. The big outer roots have to be cut off and the bigger cuts sealed.

▶ **3** Using a root hook, the finer roots are carefully teased out to give them space.

Choosing a Pot

The basic pot shapes are rectangular, oval, round, and square. These are subdivided into types of pot needed for specific kinds of plantings: shallow ovals for forest plantings, deep ovals for individual trees, different heights of square pot for cascades, and so on. The choice of color will depend on the type of tree. The tree and pot should work together in harmony. Conifers suit rust brown in a matt finish, flowering trees are complemented by a bright glaze and maples by pale cream, or, indeed, any other muted color.

When choosing a pot, make sure that it has large enough drainage holes and that any glaze is only on the outside.

The pot must be made from stoneware and have been fired to the degree necessary to prevent frost damage. Some modern, mass-produced pots can be damaged by frost, but handmade pots turned by local potters are sometimes more satisfactory. These days there are

excellent potters making good bonsai pots all over the world, so it is worth shopping around and seeing what they have to offer. The prices of handmade pots are about the same as those of imported ones, but the glazes and finishes can be better. You may also find some new designs.

LEFT As well as different shapes and sizes, pots and trays also come in a variety of colors to enhance the appearance of your bonsai.

BELOW The underside shows the pot's unique shape. I love this pot, but the patina and depth of color are not shown to their best advantage here.

ABOVE This wonderful Chinese pot is a Chugoku Chidai, or "Water Glaze," pot of perfect form, dating from 1800. It has unusually large feet set below the simple, half-curved exterior, with a triangular interior. A rich terracotta with smoked-black edges, it measures 30cm x 10cm (12" x 4").

The Key Points to Remember

● The pot should always have a clear area beneath it for ventilation and drainage of water. It is best to choose pots with feet. For pots with no feet, raise them with strips of wood to allow ventilation.

● Only repot at the correct times – early spring, well before bud break, or midfall – as long as you can protect the bonsai throughout any winter period (see troubleshooting for other times).

● Use a drainage course in deep pots, but this is not necessary in shallow pots, such as forest or group shallow-tray pots.

● Use only your fingers to push the soil in around the roots and not a chopstick, as this may damage the roots, leading to root rot and subsequent infection.

● Protect the pot from winds for at least six weeks, or until your tree has settled into its new pot. Keep it out of bright sun and heavy rain, too. Being exposed to harsh weather conditions after repotting can damage the tree when its new roots are trying to grow.

● Protect the pot in cold climates during winter.

● Plant the tree off-center in a rectangular pot.

● Do not use pots that are not frost-resistant, as these will crack in cold weather. Make sure that pots are not glazed on the interior, as the soil will be unable to adhere to the inside of the pot, which could then cause soil movement.

● Use the right type and size of pot for your bonsai.

● Make sure that you remember to put ties into the pot to secure the bonsai before you fill up the pot with soil and plant the tree.

● Understand placement of the tree in the pot. Do not finish potting if your tree is, for example, leaning backwards – a common fault.

● Do not feed the tree for at least six weeks after repotting it.

● Remember to wire in mesh to cover the drainage holes in the pot. If this is not done, the soil will fall through, leaving hollow pockets that attract wood lice, slugs, and other pests.

BELOW This magnificent pot flares out well beyond the normal rate. Although perfectly balanced, such a wide flare can result in the edges of the pot collapsing during firing. Marked with the maker's seal, it is Chinese and dates from the 18th century. Measuring 32.5cm x 25cm x 6cm (13" x 10" x 2.5"), it has cloud feet and a deeply incised, rim edge.

LEFT Deep blue, with blue on blue Moyo, this pattern depicts a mountainscape. This is a Ming dynasty earthenware pot of extremely good color and size, 25cm (10") wide and 16cm (6") high. Its deep shades are remarkable, and reflect the masterly ability of the pot-makers or glazers of this period. Such pots are rare.

ABOVE A round, 19th-century Chinese Canton Celadon glaze pot, with a plum-blossom and plum-tree design. It measures 30cm (12") across and is 21cm (8.5") deep.

LEFT A Kowatari ("Old Crossing") pot, with a wide Geho-Bachi and rim. Its beautiful Aurora Borealis design is in shades of blue Moyo. This 19th-century Quing dynasty pot is exceptionally well glazed. Its dimensions are 27cm x 29cm (11" x 12").

Potting – Quick Reference Guide

1 Cut some plastic mesh to cover the drainage holes.

2 Cut strong enough wire, 1½ or 2mm thick, for the mesh retainers. These are bent into a "Z" shape. The ends of the "Z" are bent back on themselves and are used to secure the mesh.

3 Push two (sometimes more, for a large bonsai or group) security wires, or lengths of raffia, through the outside corner holes and the mesh. I generally use 2mm anodized-aluminum wire. Leave enough wire to twist. It is helpful to slip some thin rubber or plastic tubing, like that used for automatic watering systems, over the wire. This will pad the wire against the roots as you tighten the wire to hold in the root mass.

4 If it is a deep pot, arrange a 4mm grit layer over the base. If it is shallow, then don't bother.

5 Pile the soil mix into a mound in the center of the pot if the pot is round or square, and slightly to one side if it is a rectangular or oval pot. This will create a better visual image.

6 When everything has been prepared, take your bonsai out of the old pot. Trim off about a third of the roots and remove any very large, downward-pointing roots (tap roots). Seal off these big cuts and dust them with rooting hormone powder. Do not spend too long on this or the roots will start to dry out.

7 Place the bonsai in the pot, pressing down the soil mound, and start to work the soil into the bonsai's root system.

8 Tie the security wires or raffia over the root mass, being careful not to damage or twist any of the roots. Make sure that the bonsai cannot move before adding more soil.

9 Continue to add the soil. When the soil has been worked in, add some more around the outside and stop just below the edge of the pot.

10 Water the bonsai in and leave it for a few days before watering it again. If it is hot, you may need to water it every day, but the roots will not be ready to take up water for a few days after potting. Do not feed it for about six weeks.

Case Study: A Basic Potting

1 Shape the wire to hold down the mesh that will stop the soil from falling through the base of the pot.

2 Position the ties or wires that will hold the tree in until it grows a strong root base.

3 Using your wire-mesh stays, place sufficient plastic mesh over the holes.

▼ **4** It is not always necessary, but adding a thin layer of grit to the bottom can help drainage, especially with conifers.

▶ **5** Pile the soil in a mound in the middle.

◀ **6** Put the tree on the soil mound and work the soil into the root mass. Use your fingers, as blunt tools, such as chopsticks, can damage fine roots and put the tree at risk. Using a rubber hammer (the kind used for car repairs), tap the sides of the pot a number of times to make sure that the soil is even throughout the pot.

▶ **7** Tie up the tree firmly and water it in well, then leave it for a few days. Make sure that the soil is free-draining and kept damp. Do not feed the tree for at least six weeks.

Case Study: Root-bound Nursery Material

▼ **1** In this case, the tree has been growing in an ordinary plant pot for too long.

▲ **2** The pot has to be broken in order to remove the tree safely.

◀ **3** Having been teased out, the heavy outer roots are trimmed back.

▶ **4** About 40 percent of root is removed from this *Acer*.

▼ **6** The tree is tied down over the trunk. It is important either to cover the trunk with rubber tubing at the wire areas or to watch to ensure that the bark is not marked.

▲ **5** In order to help the tree along, it was better to plant it in a growing box instead of a bonsai pot. Alternatively, a large bonsai training pot could have been used.

Growing Your Own Bonsai

There are several methods that you can use to propagate bonsai, and some are more suitable for certain species than others. This chapter looks at the main propagation techniques.

Seed

There are no such things as bonsai seeds, despite packaging claims to the contrary. Growing a

RIGHT A Japanese cedar (*Crytomeria japonica nana*) in the formal upright style.

bonsai from seed will take a long time, and it is a waste of time if you want to learn about bonsai, so buying a seedling plant is better. If you want to try growing a bonsai from seed, however, make sure that you buy suitable tree seeds from a specialist grower. There are many seed catalogs that will also contain species suitable for bonsai.

Plant the seed in commercial seed-potting compost, pure vermiculite, or any other seed culture. Water and mist it every day in the growing season to keep the soil damp. When the young seed has been growing for about six months, carefully lift out the seedling, remove the tap root, and very lightly trim the outside of the tiny new roots by a third. Replant the seedling and keep it moist, but not soggy, which will cause mildew. Repot it the following year and trim the roots again. If necessary, trim the foliage by a third. Feed it six weeks later with a quarter-strength food and repeat every week.

In the tree's third year, repeat the above procedure. Lightly wire the tree in cage-wire form and then plant it out in the garden to encourage heavier growth over the next three or four years. Remove the wire after four weeks if the tree is thickening up. Rewire the tree during the following summer for another four weeks. Depending on the species, full araining will start in the third year.

Grafting

Grafting is a technique that is mainly used on trees that do not take well to other methods. Pines are one of the best examples. Grafting can also be used to add a branch to a bare section of trunk or a twig to a bare branch area.

Case Study: Shoot Graft

▼ **1** Cut a young shoot from a branch to put into an area where there are no branches.

▼ **2** Prepare the area to receive the graft as shown. Use a sharp knife to score through the bark into the white of the cambium – the heart wood. Peel the bark back very carefully at the top and the two sides. You can slightly overestimate the size.

▶ **3** Insert the shoot and close the bark on the host over it. Cover the area with grafting tape or grafting wax (available from most nurseries). Leave for at least six months. Do not prune the new shoot for the first year, or until the graft has set.

Cuttings

Take cuttings in the spring and sprinkle them with rooting hormone powder. Plant them in sterile soil, such as cutting compost, vermiculite, or my favorite, Akadama. Hardwood cuttings are woody cuttings taken when pruning; softwood cuttings are the new shoots. Taking cuttings from any tree is fine, but some, like elms, are more resilient that others. Pines are better grafted.

Air-layering

Air-layering is a technique that is used to shorten an overlong trunk, to create a better root formation, or to make a nice trunk from a branch.

Case Study: Pine-shoot Graft

▶ **3** Prepare the area to take the shoot, in this case a branch which is a little naked and needs a twig. Cut into the branch at the same angle as that shown, but only go in about a third of its width, or 50 percent at the most.

▼ **4** Insert the shoot at the same angle and cover it with grafting tape or grafting wax. Leave it for at least nine months, keeping an eye on the graft.

▲ **1** This is a really good way in which to get an elusive bud into an area where it will not grow by any other means. Prepare the shoot in early spring from last year's new shoot.

▲ **2** Cut the end of the shoot into a spike shape, with one side having a slightly longer cut than the other. Make sure that you cut the shoot at a right angle, as it would be silly to cut a bent shoot facing into the host.

Case Study: Peg Graft

▲ **1** When a branch is needed in the trunk of a tree, bore a hole into it the same width, or a fraction smaller, than the branch.

▲ **2** Cut the end of the branch into a slight point, open the bark slightly at the end, and insert the branch into the hole. Make sure that it is a tight fit and that no cut surfaces are exposed.

▲ **3** Seal in the branch with grafting tape or grafting wax. Seal the end of the branch, too.

Leave the seal on for a year, or until the graft has taken and the shoot is growing.

Case Study: Air Layers

◀ **3** Soak some sphagnum moss in a vitamin solution of B1 – one crushed pill in 0.5l (17½ fl oz) water – or Superthrive (follow the instructions on the bottle). Press the moss firmly against the trunk as shown. I do not use rooting hormone powder, but some people do.

▲ **5** Wrap the bag in black plastic to stop light penetration.

▲ **1** Using a sharp knife, cut into the cambium just below the bark.

▶ **2** Completely remove the strip of bark. Do not leave a bridge, as this will encourage a one-sided root formation.

▲ **4** Wrap all of the moss in a clear polythene bag, so that you can check the root formation.

Keep the moss slightly damp with the vitamin solution. Check the roots after three months and look for the brown roots, not the white ones, which are not the roots that will support the tree. When the brown roots have come through, carefully transplant the tree into a seed compost and secure it by supporting the trunk. You should get a good nebari.

Styles

There are many traditional styles in bonsai, and the following examples illustrate how some of the principal styles should look. Although all of these styles are equally attractive and rewarding, fashions change in the bonsai world as quickly as in any other area of interest, and you may find that you are influenced by the current popularity of a particular style. You should always be guided by your own personal preference, however.

Leaning

(Shakan) Unlike the informal upright style, in which the trunk curves or slants slightly, for the leaning style the trunk leans at a considerable angle, mainly to one direction.

Formal Upright

(Chokkan) This is when the tree trunk is completely straight, gradually tapering towards the top. It can be a difficult style to achieve, because perfectly straight trunks are not common in nature.

Informal Upright

(Moyogi, "curved trunk") Irregular trunks with curves and twists are easier to find in nature, and this style is one of the most popular. The trunk generally follows an "S" shape.

Clump

(Kabudachi, Kabu-Buki, or Musha-Date) Clumps are formed when a number of trunks grow out of the one root mass that is above ground. As opposed to a raft that comes out of a fallen trunk, the clump grows from one solid root base.

Three Group

Group plantings are some of the most natural of the bonsai styles, as they closely emulate trees in the wild. Traditionally, trees are planted in odd numbers when there are fewer than eleven trees in total.

Five Group

A further example of group planting. This group starts to look more like a forest as the numbers increase.

Forest

(Yosue or Yosu Uye) A style using fifteen trees. Groups are generally planted to an asymmetrical design.

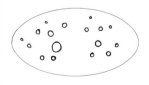

ABOVE A plan of the forest planting using fifteen trees. Here the traditional, asymmetric design can clearly be seen.

Full Cascade

(Kengai) A complicated style, the full cascade is when the tree trunk is trained to grow downwards, well below the rim of the pot. An ancient Chinese design, it is inspired by the contorted shapes of trees that cling to life in harsh terrains, such as cliff faces.

Semicascade

In this style the trunk does not grow in such an extreme manner as a full cascade. Instead it grows more horizontally.

Upright Cascade

(Otoshi Eda Kengai) This is like a traditional full cascade, but has a normal tall trunk. The top cascades down, above the edge of the pot, as opposed to a full cascade, when the trunk falls below the rim of the pot.

Single Literati

(Literati or bunjin) Inspired by the tree paintings of the most esteemed Chinese and Japanese artists (known as the Literati or bunjin), this is an elegant and sophisticated style. Literati-style trees are typified by having little foliage, as the emphasis is placed on the trunk.

Double Literati

The Literati style is based on the natural growth of trees in harsh climates, when the tree's appearance can often be stark, although beautiful.

Broom With Double Trunk

The ultimate natural-looking tree, the broom style is very popular. Most deciduous species are adaptable, as well as juniper varieties.

Broom

(Hokidachi or Hoki Zukuri) The broom style has a straight central trunk, with the branches forming into an attractive, fan-like shape.

Root Over Rock

(Ishitsuki or ishizuke) Rocks are an integral part of Japanese gardens, so it is only natural that they should have been incorporated into bonsai design. This style is often intended to emulate a mountain scene.

The Bonsai School

The aim of the Bonsai School is to introduce different methods of styling bonsai, and how spectacular results can be achieved over time. There are many other styles and techniques that you will become familiar with as you progress in your hobby, but for the purpose of this book I have chosen what I believe to be interesting examples from my own bonsai classes as teaching models that can be applied to most species.

Although I have not provided a full guide to every species, I have included detailed information on certain of the most popular varieties, and have illustrated some techniques that particularly apply to them. A reference table for the main species favored by bonsai-growers is included at the end of the chapter and provides a quick-check guide to the requirements and special considerations of each species.

Rock Planting

One of the most visually stunning methods of displaying a bonsai is to plant it on a rock. Any large rock will do, although the bigger the stone, the better the image. Fiberglass-resin rocks can also be used for lightness.

Most species of tree are suitable for rock planting. The first study illustrates what can be achieved with group plantings, using elms. The second shows a fine example of white pine.

Study 1: Elm group on rock

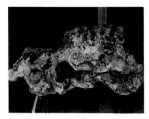

◀ 1 This was a large rock, obtained from a garden, about 1m (40") long. I washed the rock thoroughly and built up the planting areas with a clay-peat mix.

▲ 2 The overall planting scheme used seven trees. I used small-sized elms. Grown from cuttings, these trees were about six years old.

▼ 3 A close-up view of the planting. Rather than fill the entire top of the rock, I decided to use the three peak areas and to plant elms on each. It was not easy, but the result was very attractive.

Study 2: Rock Planting With White Pine

▲ **1** This is an Irish mud stone, which is fossilized mud. It is about 1m (40") in length.

▶ **2** A selection of small, grafted white pines (*Pinus parviflora*), planted on good root stock.

▲ **3** Although you can see the graft area, this will become less noticeable when the pine is older. These grafted pines are about three years old. The variety is probably *Miyajima*.

▲ **4** Prepare a peat-clay mix, 60 percent peat and 40 percent clay. Mix well.

▶ **5** Before planting, I filled in the holes in the rock with a commercial, lime-free filler paste and let it dry. I then coated the entire rock with a water-seal solution for brickwork and stone to stop the rock and the filler from breaking up or otherwise affecting the trees.

▲ **6** I had already found a good moss to apply to the planting.

▲ **7** Building a shallow wall at the top of the rock to form a low pot, I

pressed the moss into wet peat-clay mix, which sticks easily to the surface.

◀ **8** The first trees were planted and I carefully secured them to each other. The next set of trees were then installed and the entire group was secured together with wiring. This would stay in place for a year, until the group's roots had settled.

▶ **9** The completed group. The group has still to fill in, of course, but that will take another two years. The rock is in proportion to the trees and the effect gives the illusion of a small forest on a rocky escarpment.

Elm Species Information

Elms fall into a large group of trees that grow all over the world. In bonsai, we tend to use two kinds, the Chinese elm (***Ulmus parvifolia***) and the closely related Japanese gray-bark elm (***Zelkova serrata***). The latter is more commonly referred to as a zelkova, and although it is closely related to the elm (indeed, it is part of the ***Ulmaceae*** genus), it differs by having single-toothed leaves instead of the elm's double tooth.

There are many other varieties of elm that are also suitable for bonsai, including such tiny-leaved varieties as the pygmy elm, its white-edged leaves making it the "frosty" strain of the Chinese elm, and the Jacqueline Hillier elm. Although over a hundred varieties and subvarieties are available, the Chinese elm and the zelkova remain the most popular.

Starting Out

Elms are one of the few species that I am happy to recommend to grow from seed. It is better, however, to obtain seedlings, because the early work has already been done for you. Grow a dozen in a large pot or plant them outside in the garden. Simply rough-prune them for a couple of years and feed them well. Lift them out and root-prune them by 50 percent every year and then replant them. After a couple of years they will have fattened up and you can start their development as bonsai. When my little elms and zelkovas outgrow their bonsai size, I either cut them down, air-layer them, or just let them grow. They are a lovely genus to work with.

Care

Elms require the same care as any other plant – enough water, light, food, and space to grow. Elms are easy plants to grow as bonsai. Their care is simple and the bonsai techniques are very straightforward. Many elms are sold as indoor bonsai, and these are very suitable subjects. Make sure that you buy a healthy specimen, however. If

BELOW Elm trees in their natural environment. Let nature be your guide.

you buy an indoor tree, also ensure that it does not become too cold during its first year; as it is acclimatized over a two-year period.

Placement

The indoor elm tree needs air. During the winter, it must not be placed in a window whose curtains will be closed, as it may freeze at night. A light room is fine, but keep the tree away from heaters, televisions, or other heated items. Misting a tree in a heated room is very important during the winter, and you may need to mist it gently three times a day. Bathrooms are usually fine, as the air is moist. Wherever you place your bonsai, turn it around every few days to give it even light. Try to put it outside in warmer weather. If you do this, leave it out for the entire season, bringing it in late summer. Do not worry if the leaves fall off: they are meant to, and will replace themselves quickly. Indeed, defoliating an indoor bonsai, such a sageritia, will make it develop a dense crop of leaves within four weeks or so.

Outdoor elms, or acclimatized indoor elms, must be brought into a cold shelter for the winter, as the ends of the branches can get frostbite, causing the bark to die and the tips to become shriveled or white. For outdoor elms, the spring season is important, and they must receive good light. They need protection from wind, as their soft little leaves will burn. In summer, full sun is fine, but remember that if they are in small pots they will dry out quickly in hot sun, so a little shade is necessary. In autumn, elms can take anything thrown at them weather-wise, although try to prevent early frosts from getting at them.

Watering

Keep the indoor tree moist, watering it a little every three or four days, unless the soil dries out.

ABOVE A fine example of a miniature elm in summer. It is 1m (40") tall.

Make sure that you do not forget this, and do not overwater at any time, as the generally turgid air of the indoor climate does not work on the tree in the same way as if it was kept outside. Mist the tree gently when turning it every few days.

Outdoor elms need watering every two or three days in the spring, and up to twice a day in the summer. Spray them every day and watch out for mites or pests.

Feeding

Indoor trees can survive on any houseplant food. Feed them once a week throughout the spring and summer and once a month in winter. The leaves may drop after a few months in the winter, but as long as you are following the correct care regime and are checking for over- or underwatering you have nothing to worry about.

Outdoor elms need a high-nitrogen feed in the spring and a balanced feed during their mid-season. Stop feeding at the height of midsummer, when the tree enters a semidormant stage. Use low-nitrogen feed from late summer to fall to help it through the winter. The upper portion loses its leaves in fall, but the roots still grow slightly in the winter. They will continue to grow slowly as long as the roots are not frozen.

Pests and Diseases

Watch out for scale insects on variegated forms of elms. Vine weevil is becoming more common. Keep an eye open for aphids, especially black-

Study 3: Pruning and Potting an Elm

▲ 1 This is a five-year-old minibonsai that now needs branch-pruning, root-pruning, and repotting.

▶ 2 The upper portion of the elm is reduced to the required shape.

▶ 3 The roots now need to be reduced.

▲ 4 The roots are cut back by a third.

aphid attack. Use the proprietary treatments available from garden centers or bonsai nurseries. Vine weevil can be treated with nematodes.

Pruning

All types of elm can be rough-pruned like a hedge, but try to form a treelike shape. Three times a year, prune to the first set of new leaves at the crown of the tree, and to the second set at the sides. Form a triangle shape first, and fill this out as the tree develops. Use sharp scissors for this. Leaf-pruning can be done on large-leaved varieties, but is unnecessary on small-leaved trees.

Major pruning involves cutting off branches. It is important to seal the large cuts, and to make the right shape of cut, so that they will heal.

Wiring

The best time for wiring is midsummer, although it can be done in midwinter, too. Use different thicknesses of wire and be careful to remove it before the wire bites into the tree. Never wire so tightly that the wood is marked.

Potting and Root-pruning

Potting and root-pruning can be done in either early spring or midfall. However, midfall is often the better time, as many bonsai are at their most active during spring, and it is best to leave plants undisturbed unless urgent attention is required. Use an open compost, Akadama, or a mixture of both. Always use small, sharp grit for mixing into the soil, as elms need good drainage.

▼ **5** This leaves a tighter root area that can now quickly re-establish itself in a new bonsai pot.

▶ **6** The tree has now been repotted.

▶ **7** Pictured next to our elm is a similar tree that was pruned and repotted two years previously. The comparison shows how quickly elms can grow.

Study 4: Drastic Pruning

This is a slightly advanced technique, but it is not beyond anyone and will reward you with a good result.

4 The new buds were growing nicely in the second year.

▲ **1** The developer of a Jacqueline Hillier elm planted it as a seedling in 1962. I acquired it in 1985.

▶ **2** The trunk was nearly 10 cm (4") in width and the tree stood 105cm (3½ feet) high. It was a difficult tree, as the upper branches were heavy and I could not get a good look at it. I therefore took drastic action.

▶ **3** This technique was taught to me by John Naka in 1984. Cut off the top of the tree, either by air-layering, or, as in this case, with two downward cuts at differing heights. The important thing to remember is to seal the inside of the cut, then to wrap the edges tightly with raffia to stop the new buds growing out of the edge of the bark, and finally to cross your fingers. The result was excellent, and this picture shows the new growth within the second year. (I had already removed the raffia.)

▲ **5** In the third year the tree was showing great potential, and I had started to reduce the branch length and was now pruning it as described in the section on elm.

6 During the fourth year I was creating the triangle, as described earlier, and was forming the structure. The trunk was too thick and the tree was planted too high in the pot. The tree was now 60cm (24") high. It had a good, well-spaced surface root in four sections.

9 The eventual overall look. Although I would have loved to have continued developing this tree, it was stolen, and I never saw it again. You can see the way in which the tree was being shaped and how well it had responded to this technique.

7 In the fifth year I hollowed out the trunk to create an aged effect.

8 The tree pictured just before the trunk was hollowed out.

Creating a Formal Upright, Informal Upright, and Literati

Creating a traditional bonsai style is extremely rewarding, although patience is required as the tree needs a lot of time to grow fully into your desired image. These examples use pines – two needle pines, Scots pine (*Pinus sylvestris*) and black pine (*Pinus thunbergii/negra*), a Mugho pine (*Mugo*), and five white-needle pines (*Pinus parviflora*) – to show the stunning effects that can be achieved.

Study 5: Formal Upright

▲ **1** The fissured appearance of the pine bark.

▶ **2** A Scots pine in the formal upright style.

Study 6: Informal Upright

▼ **1** Another Scots pine, named "Big Bob," after Robert Porch, who found it in a nursery field.

◄ **2** The tree after three hours of wiring and shaping.

▼ **3** A year later the image had softened – I made the foliage pads less harsh.

Study 7: Literati

1 This is a collected Scots pine (*Pinus sylvestris*), 130cm (48"). It was a side branch from a bigger tree. Collected trees in this free, natural shape are called Literati or bunjin bonsai.

2 I had an idea that the Scots pine could look like this white pine.

3 This is the Literati or bunjin pine in training.

4 Three years later, I could still not decide which way I wanted to train the tree, as I was just developing the foliage at this time.

5 I eventually decided that I would make a jinn where the old trunk had been. The cambium, or bark, was healing fast, so the tree was very healthy.

▶ **6** John Naka visited me in Glasgow, Scotland, and split the trunk, dropping that part downward, into a cascade. We named the tree "Big John" after that.

▼ **9** I restyled "Big John" over a two-hour period in 1996, and apart from the lower branch the appearance was pleasant.

▼ **10** This was how "Big John" looked in 1999.

▲ **7** Seven years later, "Big John" was beginning to look like a bonsai. I had pulled the lower branch toward the trunk by this time, as the straight cascade was too stiff as it started to fill in.

▶ **8** When I moved house a few years later, the tree was left to grow a little wild.

Study 8: Styling a Twin Trunk

▲ **1** This very big shore pine (*Pinus contorta*) was the subject of a demonstration.

▼ **2** After three hours' hard work, I had found an image for it. The pot is 1m (39") long.

A beautiful example of a natural forest group of pines. This is what bonsai forest plantings aim to emulate.

White-pine Species Information

There are many varieties of white pine (*Pinus parviflora/pentaphyilla*), but all have one thing in common: the white, central, or stomatic, band down the length of the leaf (or needle). The popular white-pine bonsai come from China, Japan, or elsewhere in the Pacific Asian-rim area. They are generally styled very simply, with a twist or two in the trunk, and are invariably grafted onto a black-pine base, which is stronger.

Some varieties have very dense needle growth, while others have very short needle clusters. However, all are *Pinus parviflora*, with many various cultivars, including Kokono, Miyajima, and Brevifolia. The difference between the white pine and other pine species is that the white pine has a cluster of five needles around each bud. Scots (*Pinus sylvestris*) and black pines (*Pinus thunbergii*) have clusters of two needles, and some species, such as the red pine (*Pinus densiflora*), can have clusters of two or three needles, depending on the variety.

The white pine's natural growth habit is low and spreading, while as a bonsai it can take any shape. The common style, however, is a pyramid form, with the branches rising in clearly defined steps to the apex, or tip, of the tree.

Watering

Pines need semidry conditions in the winter, and the soil should be kept slightly damp in the growing season. Pine bonsai do not like very wet conditions. Only spray the needles from summer to early fall, in the morning and late evening.

Bud Development in Pines

In the case of white or five-needle pines, you need to trim the stronger buds, or candles, at the top of the tree first. If clusters of buds appear, remove all but two of these, to avoid your bonsai becoming too dense at the bud areas and not developing correctly. The new growth is much softer than on the two-needle Scots and black pines, and, unlike these, the five-needle pines can be pruned back quite hard after the needles have

broken. The case study demonstrates how back buds, or buds on bare branches, are created.

Bud-plucking

When pines are either collected or bought in garden centers, they invariably have long branches, with little or no twig structure. During the spring, the tree grows candles. Starting at the bottom of the tree, or at the weaker, lower branches, pluck out 50 percent of the candle with your fingers, holding the bottom with one hand to stop it from breaking off. (Leave all obviously weak buds alone. If the branch has only weak buds, wait until they have swollen. If this has not occurred by early summer or late spring, then get to work on the other branches.) A week later, pluck the next layer of branches in the same way, and thus work your way up to the, by now, vigorous top area. The smaller second bud will soon grow and, again using both hands, hold the base of bud and pluck out 50 percent of the second bud.

The reason for bud-plucking Scots and all two-needle pines is that the stronger growth is at the top of the tree, and if you started to pluck there, all of the tree's energy would be directed to that point to repair the damage. This would divert

BELOW A little black pine (*Pinus thunbergii*).

BELOW Sunset and pine.

energy from the weaker areas, which could result in eventual growth loss within these areas.

However, the reverse is necessary when pruning five-needle pines. In this case, you start at the top, instead of the bottom, because the tree is less likely to abort its weaker, lower branches. The important thing to look out for is the formation of twin buds. Pluck out the longer bud and wait until the smaller bud has grown longer than the plucked bud. Then remove the first bud and reduce the new bud by half, following the same weekly regime. As long as the tree is healthy, never leave more than two buds on any growth point. The tree will then develop new buds along the branches.

Needle-plucking

This procedure is a little more advanced, but you may like to be aware of it. Do not allow more than two buds to grow from any one point. If this happens, simply pluck out the soft needles on the extra buds. After you have needle-plucked during the following growing season, you will probably have little pockets of dense clusters of buds (called "witches' brooms"). You must therefore reduce this multiple growth to the one or two buds that are important in your overall plan.

Watering After Bud-plucking Pines

Be sure to water the pine well between plucking, as you are hoping for vigorous growth. If you withhold water at this crucial time, you will reduce the needles, but at the expense of ramification. Never reduce the needles until you have structure, as the tree will not have sufficient ability to photosynthesize or develop its root structure, so have patience. If you pot your pine

Study 9: Bud Development in Pines

▲ 1 The long needles of a normal pine.

▶ 3 In the third year, small buds will develop on the older wood. Make sure that you remove the terminal, or end, bud from the branch, or else the sap will bypass the smaller bud in favor of the stronger, terminal bud.

▶ 2 After breaking the long buds in half during the first year, in the second year, the pine will show many more buds in spring.

▲ 4 By the fourth year, the pine will have a dense mass of foliage.

in a classic pine soil, which is well drained and porous, with no more than 40 percent organic material, you will help the roots to develop correctly. However, in countries that have a lot of rain, tilt the pot on a small piece of wood to drain away the water. Remember to change the direction of the tilt in severely inclement weather, as water can collect in one corner of the pot.

To Remove or Not to Remove the Leader Buds?

After new buds have developed, keep the leader bud at the end of that branch short, or the sap will bypass the new bud to feed the strongest bud. You can remove the entire leader bud if you have strong back buds, but be very careful if these buds are weak, or you will lose the entire branch or twig. During spring, you can then continue to pluck out all of the center buds on the branches whose length you are happy with. This in turn develops fine twigs.

Pests and Diseases

Aphids, adelgids, mealy bugs, red spider mites, and lopho (*Lophodermium pinastre*, a pine-needle cast) are all potential villains. If pests arrive, treat the pine with systemic. Lopho is a fungus, and is treated with a copper fungicide in a weekly dose for five or six weeks.

Lopho is identified by lateral yellow stripes on the needle and affects mainly pines. Adelgids look like wooly fluff between the needles. Systemic will kill the creature, but use a concentrated hose spray to wash away the fluff.

It is important to note that when using any fungicide on a tree, do not allow any to get on to the soil. Cover the soil with a polythene sheet or plastic bag and then a towel. Fungicide will

5 When the tree is ready and styled, you can reduce the needles by using a number of methods. One is to reduce the pine's water intake during the time that the needles are emerging from the candles. Only do this on a healthy tree, and one on which the styling has been completed. Smaller needles mean that the tree is not growing as fast as a normal tree.

▼ **6** Here is an example of bud development. This tree has a rough shape, but no definition.

▼ **7** After three years, the tree has grown into shape, due to the increase in new buds.

damage the beneficial mycelium fungus that helps the roots to grow.

Feeding

Use manufactured fertilizers at half strength. In the spring, feed young trees with a high-nitrogen fertilizer; in summer, with a balanced fertilizer, and in early fall with a low-nitrogen fertilizer. Feed every three weeks at the beginning of the season, and every four weeks from early summer through to the end of fall.

Using fertilizers at full strength is particularly dangerous for established trees, as the roots are very tender and may suffer from being fed. You do not want lush, juvenile growth, so feed them with low-nitrogen fertilizer until early summer. Use a balanced feed in summer and return to a low-nitrogen fertilizer in fall. Feed mature trees approximately every five to eight weeks.

BELOW Most pine branches grow upwards in nature. Only the tips point downwards.

Pruning

Prune the old needles at the rear of each bud's needle cluster every three years. Leave only two buds at each tip, depending on the health of the tree. If the tree is weak, leave three buds. If you want to develop young, inner buds along the branch, then prune out some, if not all, of the leading tips that aren't required.

White pine: start cutting candles from the top of the tree by half to two-thirds, and work your way down each week until you reach the bottom layer of branches. The strongest bud at the top of the tree will grow. Scots pine: do not prune the buds up and down the tree at the same time because this will exhaust the tree. It is better to pull the soft, new needles out of the sheath every three years, because this forces the tree to create shorter needles the following year.

As the tree starts to shape up over the next three or four years, look at the inner buds on each branch, and when bud-plucking, start plucking the inner buds first. After five days, pluck the outer buds, and start on the next upper layer a week later. Although this will increase the plucking time by 75 percent, you will soon see the difference.

Maintenance-pruning of buds is done when the tree is complete, and uses the basic plucking technique of plucking one layer of branches at a time, covering all of the buds on each layer at the same time and progressing upwards each week.

Soil Type

A free-draining soil is important for all pines, and should consist of five parts 2–3mm grit to three parts organic matter, such as a mixture of peat, leaf mold, or even composted bark. Speak to your bonsai-seller, or to other local bonsai-growers, and they will advise you on the best soil for your climate. To retain moisture, trees in hot climates may need a little more organic soil than trees in colder or wetter climates.

Light/Shade Requirements

Pines, junipers, and larch like some shade for part of the day during the summer and should be kept in as light an area as possible, free from winter climatic problems, during the cold months. In most cases, full sun may make the tree more yellow in some cases, while full shade (not advised) will force the dark-green or glaucus to emerge. Balance its light requirements and you will have a healthy tree.

Repotting

Repot young trees every three years and mature trees every five years. Use a rust, brown, gray, or deep-blue colored pot for conifers. I prefer matt, dark-brown pots made by local potters, and it is wise to support them, as they can quickly make a pot to your requirement; although expensive, imported Japanese pots are also nice. Larger bonsai nurseries generally have a very good variety of stock. When buying a pine, check that it has the beneficial mycelium fungus, and always make sure that there are no root aphids.

Using Nursery Trees or Garden Center Material for Bonsai

Bonsai can be readily bought from nurseries and garden centers, and buying more mature trees can offer a quicker route to creating wonderful styles. Studies 10 and 11 use a Meyers juniper (*Juniperus squamata meyeri*), which was large stock obtained from a landscape nursery.

Meyers juniper is a blue-green juniper with needle-scale foliage that can be a little prickly when you are training it. Every time you are about to work with this material you should therefore spray it with water, which softens the needles. Otherwise wear a pair of latex or leather gloves. I wear rubber gloves almost all of the time when I work with junipers or other species that may cause slight irritation. These details can be applied to almost any variety of juniper.

Study 10: Creating a Juniper Group

▶ **3** The spiky nature of needle-juniper types can make wiring and plucking painful. Spray the tree with water before you work on it and the needles will soften.

▼ **4** By the third year, the group had started to fill in.

▲ **1** Stripping the top off the tree reduces its height. Cut slightly upwards, and then pull down the opposite side to create a sharp apex of wood. It should look like a natural tree top that has been struck by lightning.

▶ **2** After rough styling, this is a group of such trees after one year.

Study 11: Creating a Juniper Formal Upright

4 I removed four branches to reduce the bulk of the tree and started developing the foliage pads by plucking the tips out every two months.

▲ **1** Creating a formal upright was another project that I worked on with this species.

▶ **2** Reducing its height still made this tree 130cm (50") high. The first styling was intended to establish the overall shape for its health, as well as its style.

▲ **3** Three years later, the tree's foliage had been established.

▲ **5** A year later, the tree was starting to resemble the pine image that I had been planning.

◀ **6** I went too far with the plucking, and as a result the tree was now too stiff in appearance.

7 The following year, I reduced another branch and softened the image.

8 In the same year, I tidied up the foliage pads and put the tree on display. It still looked a little stiff, however. I prefer to create a natural, slightly destructured image.

9 By the following year, 1999, I had established the softness that I was looking for and the tree was now starting to become a bonsai. Its style is meant to emulate a Scots-pine image.

Stage 2 from now on will be to remove the lower branch and tidy the foliage pads and apex.

Correcting Design and Growth

Sometimes you will need to take action to correct a tree that is growing unevenly.

The first example (Study 12) shows the styling of a Norway spruce (*Picea abies*). Studies 13 and 14 look at correcting maples (*Acer buergirianum* and *Acer dissectum*).

have used large material in order to show clearly what can be achieved by wiring.

Study 12: Correcting Spruce Design

▲ **1** As you can see, the foliage is really only growing on one side. The trunk and nebari are good, so it was decided to develop the foliage around the other side. In nature, this view would be of the back of the tree, as this side had been in shade and foliage grows towards the sunlight.

▲ **4** This is the back of the tree when it was completed.

◀ **3** After removing a few unnecessary branches, I used them to make jinns, which I inserted as grafts into the area of the trunk that was devoid of any growth or structure.

▲ **5** This is the side view.

▲ **2** The front of the tree is a mass of branches, but these are mainly quite thin.

◀ **6** This is the preferred front view. The styling took about four hours, with four people doing the wiring. Its farther development now simply involves plucking the foliage tips to encourage a better structure. After a couple of years, when the tree has settled, it will be planted into a gray or russet, oval pot.

Study 13: Correcting a Maple

▲ **1** I lifted this *Acer dissectum* from a garden after the owner, who was selling her house, said that I could have it. I cut off all of the foliage and started from scratch.

▼ **2** Two years later, the first shaping had begun.

▲ **3** After four years, the tree was well on its way to becoming a bonsai. In this photograph it stands at over 1m (40") high.

Study 14: Correcting a Trident Maple Styling With a Mature Tree

▲ **1** This trident maple was imported as a stump, without any branches, from Japan. It took nine years for it to achieve this shape.

▶ **2** In winter, the branch definition is a joy to behold.

It is possible to create an attractive bonsai by carefully styling a mature, full-sized tree. This involves cutting down and repotting the tree, followed by drastic branch-structure redevelopment.

The case studies, which each use maple varieties, illustrate the redevelopment of mature trees into bonsai forms.

Study 15 shows the cutting and styling of a group of maples (*Acer palmatum*). The trees – fourteen of them – were in a field that was due to be redeveloped for housing in 1987. The maples had been planted from seed in 1945.

Study 15: Styling Mature Maples

▲ **1** These are the trees in their original setting.

▶ **2** When I got them home, I was a little concerned about the scale of the task. Maples can be cut right back to the stump, and this had to be done simply to fit them into their containers.

▶ **4** We will now look at one tree's development over the following ten years. It had to be trimmed back completely to enable me to start all over again.

▼ **5** Year 1: I cut off all of the main branches. It was hard to believe that this would ever be a bonsai!

▲ **3** Using a 50-50 mix of grit and potting compost, we planted them into large buckets. Six months later, they had started to sprout.

▲ **6** I hollowed out the edges of the cuts so that the cambium (bark) would grow over them correctly, without creating a lumpy edge.

▼ **7** Two years later, the tree was budding all over the trunk.

▼ **8** This is the tree after four years. The branches now need placement, as they are too wide.

◀ **9** After wiring, the tree now has a bonsai shape. This took three hours.

▼ **10** After nine years the bonsai has come of age in 1997.

▲ **11** Although it is a little large for a bonsai, in 1998 it is still a very impressive tree.

Maple Species Information

FAR RIGHT A maple (*Acer palmatum*) over rock.

If pines are considered to be the kings of bonsai, then surely the glorious maples must be the queens. I grow all types of maples in all sorts of styles, and achieve deep and detailed ramification using reasonably simple techniques.

RIGHT An informal upright maple (*Acer buergerianum*).

The species that are the easiest to work on are the green-leaved types, such as the pure Japanese maple (*Acer palmatum*) and trident maple (*Acer buergerianum*). The Yatsubusa varieties are more delicate, and I suggest that you do not leaf-prune these types unless you are sure that they can take it. Varieties such as *Acer palmatum atropurpureum* are sometimes weak and difficult to back-bud. Do not leaf-prune the deep-red to purple color group. You can develop this variety through bud-pinching.

Kiyohime are by nature very dense, but as they are stronger at the sides keep the side growth down or the upper portion will die back, leaving you with a bald tree. All maples will leaf-burn if you put them out into the windy weather of spring, so you should wait until the soft leaf becomes firm and hard. Keep them in a sheltered area away from wind, if possible.

From a Prostrate Tree to an Informal Upright

When choosing your bonsai style, you may find that you need, or want, to change the direction of the tree's growth. This case study illustrates this technique using a juniper (*Juniperus procumbens*).

The Maple's Year

EARLY SPRING: Although you can repot at almost any time, this is the optimum period for the majority of maples. Kashima and Kiyohime will have started to spread at this time, so make sure that they are protected. Feed 0-10-10 (zero nitrogen) every seven days to stop lush growth, but only after the buds have opened.

THROUGHOUT SPRING: Start plucking out the bud centers.

EARLY SUMMER: After the first two feeds, start giving them a high-nitrogen feed to build up stamina in young trees. If you want good fall color, cut down the high-nitrogen food. If the tree is healthy, consider a full or partial defoliation, which can be followed by selective wiring. The tree should be looked after as during spring. The problem with summer defoliation is sunburn rather than winds.

MIDSUMMER: Wire trees with cage (not tight) or protected wire, and carry out any major pruning at this time of summer dormancy. Reduce feeding until late midsummer.

LATE SUMMER: Start feeding weekly with low-nitrogen food. This is the last opportunity for defoliation before fall.

EARLY FALL: Trim any leaves that are growing out of the planned shape. Stop feeding if the leaves start to change color. Good fall color is achieved with little or no nitrogen feed. The question is whether or not you want to risk the tree's health for a short-term benefit. It is probably better to wait until the tree has been completed and then to reduce the feed to zero nitrogen for one year.

MIDFALL: Complete your feeding program with low- or zero-nitrogen feed.

LATE FALL/EARLY WINTER: Remove any dead leaves and make sure that the trees are protected against winter frosts and wind.

WINTER: This is the other time when you can perform major surgery on your bonsai.

Study 16: From Prostrate Tree to Informal Upright

▲ **1** This is a *Juniper procumbans* grown in a cascade style. The owner, Noel Plowman, wanted me to refine it a little.

▶ **2** I studied it for a few minutes and realized that a classical bonsai was in there somewhere. All I needed to do was to put it in an upright position and find the structure.

▶ **4** Serious wiring took place next. Noel was not entirely convinced at this stage.

◀ **3** I trimmed about 40 percent of the foliage to find the branch structure.

◀ **5** After two hours, the shape was starting to emerge. This a view of the completed back of the bonsai.

▼ **6** This is a view of the completed front. After three hours of work we had created a very attractive image. Noel made a pot for the tree in the following year and it now takes pride of place in his collection.

Bonsai in the Forest Style

When creating bonsai, the aim is to recreate perfectly in miniature a tree that you would find in the wild. This intention can be seen to particularly stunning effect within the forest, or group, style, in which proportion and perspective are used to create a realistic miniforest scene. When correctly sized and placed, the trees can mirror a tree-grouping in nature. Larger trees placed at the front will appear smaller to the viewer, while smaller trees at the back will give the illusion of distance and of large trees in that distance.

When viewed close up, or in a photograph with no frame of reference, there is usually nothing to distinguish a group of miniature bonsai from a natural, full-sized forest.

Most species are suitable for forest styling.

Study 17: Forest style With Hackberry (*CELTIS*)

▲ **1** This is a typical example of a hackberry.

▲ **2** This photograph shows how massive the trunks of hackberry bonsai can be.

▶ **3** I was on a tour in South Africa with an American bonsai master, Roy Nagatoshi, who was curious about what I was planning.

▼ **4** I started sorting out the various sizes of hackberries that I found in Rob Clausen's yard. Rob is one of South Africa's leading bonsai masters.

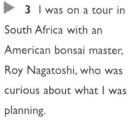

◀ **5** I prepared the plants by removing the excess soil and reducing the length of the roots in readiness for planting. They were then temporarily transplanted into shallow containers.

▲ **6** Rob checking that the transplanting has been done correctly.

▼ **7** The completed forest, styled in the form of a veldt image. Rob made the huge, 2m, 40cm x 90cm (8ft x 3 ft) pot with a steel base and wooden sides. He also made a special table on which to display the entire unit.

◀ **8** A close-up view of the inside of the group, showing how realistic it is. The entire planting took me about four hours.

Study 18: Cedar Group 1

This is a cedar group that I created in Italy. It is 2m (6ft) long.

▲ **1** Carmelo Romano and Eugenio Zardi, the organizers of the Imola Bonsai Club, stand beside the group. The group was styled in the shape of an Italian mountain forest and was named "Don Umberto, 'Protector' of Imola," a tongue-in-cheek reference to a very famous forest created by John Naka, called "Goshin, Protector of the Forest."

▲ **2** Two of the central trees that were prepared before the demonstration.

▲ **3** This is the same group after three years. The central forest is now very attactive, as the foliage pads are developing well. The middle and smaller groups are perspective plantings and still need some work. The entire planting is starting to look quite realistic. It will take another three years to complete.

▼ **4** A detail of the forest floor.

Study 19: Cedar Group 2

This is another cedar group that I created at the first Italian Joint Clubs Convention.

◀ **3** I made this two years after the previous group. Members of the clubs that I was a regular demonstrator at joined me in preparing the material. In this way I completed the group in two hours.

▲ **1** Material for my demonstration.

▶ **2** Eugenio and another Imola Bonsai Club member created this slab.

◀ **4** A close-up view of the forest floor.

Study 20: Mixed Group – Perspective Planting

This study shows the making of another large forest planting using elms (*Ulmus*) and Zelkova. I wanted to explore the idea of perspective in a narrow space. This group of different kinds of trees took over four hours to complete. The forest was over 30cm (14") wide by 3m (12ft) long.

▲ **1** The slab was made by Bill Jordan, who is seen helping me to prepare the material for planting. It is made from chicken wire and fiberglass resin.

▶ **2** Every tree was wired into the slab and planted dry. The foliage was constantly sprayed.

▲ **3** The completed group was over 3m (12ft) long. The idea was that planting smaller groups on the same level, but at the back of the slab, would give perspective to the planting and make these smaller groups look as if they were a long way off. The larger group at the front was to be the image of a nearby forest, and the middle-sized group a middle-distance, and the small group a far-distance, image. It took four hours of work to design and plant.

▲ **4** I always show the detail that I insist on when viewed up close, as well as from a distance. I like to create realistic-looking landscapes.

Larch Species Information

The very beautiful larch, or *Larix*, varieties are the staple material of bonsai-growers the world over. Japanese larch is more delicate than its European sister, and the larger collected specimens tend to be European. A deciduous, monoecious species, the branches grow in irregular whorls. The leaves are straight and develop from tight rosettes on the short branch spurs that grow on older wood and in bunches on short, red, side shoots and on young growing shoots. They are arranged in spirals. The color is bright lime green at the start of the season, bright to dark green during the summer and yellow in the fall.

Varieties

There are many varieties of larch, from the common European larch (*Larix decidua*) to the exotic Himalayan larch (*Larix griffithiana*). The most popular larch for bonsai cultivation is the Japanese larch (*Larix kaempferi*). It has a simple growth pattern that is easily exploited by the bonsai-grower. There is also a species from north-western America called *Larix lyallii*, which grows as a short, dense shrub in its natural shape and is accepted as an alpine form of larch.

Collecting

In many regions, the common larch has great popularity as bonsai. Some of the trees that I have either worked on, or seen, in collections are quite massive and attractive, but the only way in which to obtain a fine, large, ancient larch is to collect it from the wild. The problem is that many collected trees do not survive their first or second year. I suggest that you first gain experience through growing nursery stock and then go collecting with an experienced bonsai-grower. Listen to their advice on proper and safe collecting techniques. Always remember to ask permission from the owner of the land before collecting any tree.

Study 21: Restyling an Outgrown Established Larch

▼ **1** The restyle begins.

▶ **2** Trimming out the foliage.

▲ **3** Making jinns.

▲ **4** The restyle complete. It took two hours.

Aftercare of a Collected Tree

Daily spraying with a light mist will soon settle the tree and stop transpiration. The problem that collectors have when lifting a larch is that the tree has a tendency to collapse in the first or second year. One of the main reasons for this is that they overwater the tree instead of simply misting it. Misting every day and watering only when the soil begins to dry will let the tree settle gently. A 50-50 mix of peat and grit added to the existing soil is all that is needed, as this soil is free-draining and does not retain water on the surface.

If the tree remains healthy, start feeding it two months after it has settled down. Keep it out of strong sunlight for the first three months and always out of wind. Cats and dogs, attracted by the "freshly dug" smell, should be kept away.

I mention the use of existing soil because the larch, like the pine, has beneficial mycelium fungus in its root area, and this "symbiotic" fungus helps to maintain the health of the tree and encourages more growth at the root and upper levels. The fungus looks a little like cream-colored cotton-wool thread. Always watch out for root aphid, as it is easy to mistake for mycelium at a first glance. Root aphid looks like blue-white cotton-wool thread, and if you look closely you will see tiny, white, oval aphids clustering about.

Study 22: Larch Group – Five Trees

▲ 1 These are ten-to-fifteen-year-old, forestry-stock Japanese larches (*Larix kaempferi*) obtainable around the world from nurseries. Setting them into a rough shape and pruning out the excess branches. Always do this before cutting the roots and planting them.

▲ 2 Trimming out the excess growth before planting. I do not do this very much as it depends on the species.

▶ 3 Place them in a large training – Mica – pot. Always tie them firmly into place.

▲ 4 Let the growth grow wild for two years and then cut back the new growth to the first set of buds on the new growth in the second year only. Do not prune at any other time during the first two years. Feed the trees heavily to force growth.

Remove as many as you can and then treat the whole root system with a systemic-insecticide bath for about thirty minutes.

Buying

Buying a larch from a nursery is usually expensive, but if you find a commercial nursery you can pick up a few dozen seedlings at a reasonable cost. Buying a collected larch is also possible from the larger bonsai nurseries or from a bonsai exhibition – ask your local club for details of events. Some of the specialist nurseries occasionally import fine-specimen bonsai from Japan (***Larix kaempferi***) or China (***Larix potanii***),

but expect to pay a lot for them. Most nurseries have grown good-quality Japanese larch trees for a number of years, however. They grow quite quickly, and if you start with a decent-sized tree you can have a nice bonsai in less than five years.

Watering

If it is healthy, water your larch every day during the growing season, but be careful that it does not become waterlogged. One method that I use is to reduce the outer 20 percent of the soil around the perimeter of the pot and then replace it with a well-draining soil containing some water-

▼ **5** After two years, and having been cut back, this is the group in the third year.

▲ **6** It has now been transplanted. The tree is just starting to develop finer twigs.

◄ **7** The top was too tall, so I jinned it back. This is how the tree looks in the fourth year.

▲ **8** The jinn is still too tall, so that was reduced in the fifth year.

◄ **9** I had noticed many such images in nature.

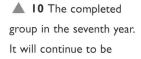

▲ **10** The completed group in the seventh year. It will continue to be

developed over the next few years.

ABOVE A collected larch.

The Larch's Year

LATE WINTER/EARLY SPRING: Protect the larch from severe weather conditions. Either cover it up or keep it close to the house. Repot it in early spring.

SPRING: When buds are coming out, start to feed it every week at full strength to force the growth. This regime is reduced only when the tree is more or less finished, when food reduction is used to maintain its shape. This is the time for aphids and adelgids, so watch the tree carefully, because the aphid could destroy an otherwise healthy tree. This is the time to view the little rosebuds of larch leaves.

LATE SPRING: Continue to feed the tree and start to pluck or break the long growth that is starting to form, working from the top down.

MIDSUMMER: Do not feed the tree.

LATE SUMMER: Start to reduce feeding to every two weeks and use a balanced food e.g., an equal amount of N.P.K. Change the feed again to a low- or zero-nitrogen combination like 0-10-10, or use tomato fertilizer. Stop pruning until winter to enable the tree add to its strength before the dormant period.

MIDFALL: When the tree changes its lime-green color to a brilliant yellow, it rewards you for any trouble that may have given you by looking really lovely.

LATE FALL: Protect the tree from frosts, winds, and overwintering insects that may want to spend their vacation in your larch. After the needles have fallen, spray the foliage with a systemic insecticide.

EARLY WINTER: Proceed as for late fall, but reduce watering to almost nothing if your tree is being kept under cover. Water only if the tree needs it. I water about once a month during this period. The rain caters for trees left outside, and a wedge-shaped block of wood placed under the pot will allow excess water to drain away.

MIDWINTER: This is a good time to plan what you are going to do regarding pruning, and to try to visualize the desired eventual shape.

---

holding material. This may seem contradictory, but the tree needs moisture in order to grow and slightly damp is better than absolutely dry soil. Use a mix of 50-50 Akadama and peat or 50-50 2mm grit and peat, leaving the original soil near the middle of the tree to retain the mycelium fungus. This results in looser, free-draining soil.

In the winter, when it is wet or cold, little water is required, but in spring the watering is increased to a daily routine. In warmer climates, such as the mountain regions of France, Italy, or Spain, the natural trees get little water for up to three months, resulting in a tougher bark and shorter needle growth. I normally reduce watering to every second day in the middle of the summer for three weeks to make the tree work for every drop that it gets, thus encouraging shorter needle growth and a more corky bark.

Feeding

When young needles have opened, feed your larch with a full-strength, high-nitrogen fertilizer in spring. During summer, reduce the feed, but use a balanced fertilizer. Then use a low- or zero-nitrogen fertilizer until the needles begin to turn yellow in fall. This will achieve growth in exactly the way that you want. All larch buds grow in a twist around the twig. In late winter, cut back to the last buds of the last year's growth, but leave a bud growing in the direction that you want the new growth as the terminal bud on each twig – "directional bud-pruning."

Repotting a Group

Repotting a group of larches does not mean dismantling them. Simply trim the outside edges of the group planting by about 10 to 20 percent

LEFT Cut growth back to the first set of buds.

all of the way round. The best time to do this is in early spring. The colors of the pots should be gray, rust, brown or dark-yellow, ocher shades.

Year-by-year Pruning for Shape and Density

Wait until the leaves have dropped and the bonsai is in dormancy before pruning it. The best time for this is mid- to late winter. Pruning simply requires pinching out the new growth at the tip of each branch or bud all over the tree. Do this in late spring and, if growth is very vigorous, late summer or early fall.

Pruning an Established Two-year-old Tree in a Pot

Year 1: Cut back to the first set of buds on the previous year's growth. Look carefully at the way in which the buds are pointing and rub off the bud opposite the one that you wish to grow.
Year 2: Do the same, but allow the branch to grow a little. On the bottom branch, cut back to

the third set of buds and rub off the opposite bud. On the middle group of branches, cut back to the second set of buds and repeat. On the top section, or apex, cut back to the first set of buds. Years 3 and 4: Repeat as for year 2.

Restyling a Large Tree Into a Small Bonsai

If a tree has grown too tall, it will need restyling to create a good bonsai image. Study 23 illustrates the styling of an over-tall box (*Buxus sempevirens*).

Refining your Bonsai

You will sometimes find that your bonsai or penjing has grown, or is growing, out of shape. In this case you will need to undertake some refining work to restore the tree's correct image. Studies 24 to 29 give examples of how different varieties can lose their definition and how this problem can be corrected.

ABOVE The larch will grow long shoots.

Study 23: Restyling a Large Tree Into a Small Bonsai

▼ **2** I removed the top, as I had noticed that the base was quite interesting. This side is quite bare.

▲ **1** This box was too tall and the trunk was very stiff. It is hard to bend box without snapping it when it gets to this size. I needed thin, small stems to work with.

▲ **3** This is the other side of the base, which is far more attractive.

▶ **4** I carved out the bare side.

▲ **5** I completed the styling using the smaller, finer shoots that will later strengthen into shape. The foliage will completely cover the apex after three years and will then require simple pruning to maintain the shape.

Study 24: Refining a Hemlock (*TSUGA*)

▼ **2** I removed the long apex and then pruned away a little of the length. The reshaping took about two hours.

▲ **1** This tree had been styled a few years previously, but was now growing too long.

▲ **3** After wiring the tree into shape, I had a better-balanced image.

Study 25: Refining a Collected Bonsai

▼ 1 This is a large larch (*Larix*) without any shape. It has been growing on a stone slab.

▶ 2 I spent about three hours wiring it. Although this is not the finished bonsai, the wiring gives the tree a design that can be worked on.

Study 26: Refining and Defining a Tree

▲ 1 I needed to retain all of the foliage in order to redesign this black pine (*Pinus thunbergii*).

▶ 2 After wiring the tree thoroughly, I was able quickly to define the shape and restore it to its bonsai status.

Study 27: Refining Nursery Stock

▲ 1 This hemlock (*Tsuga*) had been roughly shaped into a bonsailike design, but now needed extensive pruning and wiring in order to find the style within it.

▲ 2 After wiring and pruning, the tree was staring to look a little more like a bonsai. The branches were very long, so I created the shape by lifting up the longer branches and dropping the existing foliage pad.

Study 28: Collected Material

▲ 1 A yew (*Taxus*) that has been in a box for three years. It is nearly 75cm (30") tall.

▶ 2 An hour later I had the beginnings of an attractive bonsai.

▼ 3 An example of a collected yew after a year.

Study 29: One-sided Growth

▶ 1 Simon Misdale worked with me on this tree. I realized that the cypress (*Chamaecyparis*) had only two branches and that it was going to be very hard to create a design using its height. The tree was also covered in lichens, which, although they indicate clean air, also represent a pest on local growers' bonsai. Lichens must be removed every month by hand.

▼ 2 By removing the upper portion I was able to work on the lower branch and thus create a more defined image.

Growing a Bonsai From a Seedling to an Adult Tree

Although you can create a bonsai from nursery stock or collected trees, there is something particularly rewarding about growing a bonsai from a young seedling. It does take patience, however, as the completed tree can take years to develop.

Study 30 shows the development of my first tree, a dwarf cypress (***Chamaecyparis pisifera compacta nana***).

The name of this tree is "Ascot Lady." You will discover why.

Study 30: From Seedling Tree to Adult

◀ **3** As the tree grew during the third year, I repotted it into a bigger pot. At this point I was plucking the foliage without following any plan.

▼ **4** In the fourth year, I had too many branches and learned to make a jinn. I found another pot, too.

▲ **1** This was my first attempt at wiring back a tree during the early 1970s. I managed to bend the trunk and some branches, although I was not sure where, or why I was doing this. I had just read about wiring and wanted to try it, so I used a very cheap seedling about three years old. It was about 5cm (12") high.

▶ **2** In the second year the weird shape that I had managed to achieve was growing in well.

5 In the fifth year, I was actively working on a plan, but was beginning to notice that the shape of the tree distinctly resembled a female figure.

6 By the sixth year, I had developed a dense branch structure and the female shape was becoming increasingly apparent.

7 The back was sticking out, so I removed the foliage on the front branch and started work on the apex.

8 The "Ascot Lady," with her huge Ascot hat, holding her fan in her hand behind her.

9 The other side is certainly more treelike. The "Ascot Lady" measures 60cm (24") in height and 80cm (29") in length.

Styling a Bonsai Over a Long Period

Developing your bonsai into one of the traditional styles requires patience, as the image may take many years to complete. However, the finished result is well worth the wait, as the following studies show. See pages 74-77 for more examples of traditional styles.

Study 31: Developing a Formal Upright Over Twenty Years

▲ 1 *Cryptomeria* in 1980.

▶ 2 This is the same tree in 1996.

▶ 3 The same tree in 2000. The tree has filled out in this picture, as the owner is now allowing the foliage pads to become a little thicker.

Study 32: Developing a Twin Trunk Over Twenty Years

▲ 1 One side of a twin-trunk needle juniper (*Juniperus rigida*) in 1980.

▶ 2 The same side in 2000.

▲ 3 The other side, pictured in 1980.

▶ 4 The same side, pictured in 2000.

Study 33: Styling a Collected Pine (PINUS SYLVESTRIS)

▲ **1** Collected from the mountains of Scotland, this pine's trunk measures 12.5cm (5") across.

▼ **2** Three years later, the tree is starting to achieve some shape. I still could not get the lower branch to work properly, however.

▲ **3** Peter Adams and I worked on the tree for a number of years, and it was starting to achieve some definition.

▼ **4** The completed tree after ten years, at 1m (40") tall.

Flowering Trees

Many trees are collected for their wonderful color when in bloom. These include wistaria, bougainvillea, apple trees (**Malus**), and many more. I have chosen three of my own favorite species.

Satsuki Azalea (Rhododendron indicum)

Satsuki means "fifth month" in Japanese, when most flowering azaleas come into bloom.

PLACEMENT: Keep your azalea in a light place, but out of bright sun.

WATERING: Water it every day during the growing season. It likes a lot of humidity, so mist it two or three times a day – more in hot weather.

FLOWERS: In the fifth and sixth months.

FEED: Feed your azalea from late spring, but stop before the flowering buds have swelled to half-size. Use an ericaceous feed.

POTTING AND SOIL: Repot the azalea every year after flowering, or in late winter before full bud growth. Repot young plants every year and older bonsai every three to four years. It has fine thread roots, so be careful when removing the soil. It will stand severe cutting-back if it is healthy. Use a lime-free soil, 60 percent organic and 40 percent grit, or the Japanese Kanuma soil.

PRUNING: The azalea can be pruned after flowering. It can also be pruned back severely to the stump to achieve a heavier trunk shape.

PROBLEMS: In order not to tire the tree, as they start to swell, pluck out the flower buds every three years. This will encourage more green leaves and subsequent vigor.

Apricot (Prunus)

Apricot, or **Prunus mume,** is a scented flowering shrub that blooms in late winter when it has no leaves. The flowers can be white, red, and pink. Apricots rarely have excellent twig structures, other than the shoots that hold the flowering

BELOW A fabulous cascade azalea in John Naka's garden.

older bonsai every three years. Use a 60 percent organic and 40 percent grit-based soil.

PRUNING: It can be pruned after flowering. Prune back growth in fall by half, or to shape, but look for flowering shoots.

PROBLEMS: Apricots need sun.

Hawthorn (*Crataegus*)

PLACEMENT: Keep your hawthorn in a light place, with bright sunlight, if possible.

LEFT Another azalea, but with a more slender, informal appearance.

BELOW A beautiful apricot in the informal upright style.

buds. The trunks are usually rough, and can be carved to emulate old, gnarled trees. Young trees (sold in many nurseries) can be grafted.

PLACEMENT: Keep your apricot in bright sun, or as sunny a place as you can (it is not a good subject for dull climates). Watch out for late frosts, as this tree, like many species, will be damaged by die-back caused by frost. The flowering buds will abort or, at best, if the remaining buds do flower they will stress the frost-damaged tree.

WATERING: Water your apricot every day during the growing season. It likes a lot of humidity, so mist it two or three times a day – more in hot weather. Keep the soil moist in winter, when the flowers are developing.

FLOWERS: Late winter, but let the tree grow wild in summer.

FEED: Every two weeks during the mid-growing season only.

POTTING AND SOIL: Repot yearly in late winter, before half-bud growth. Pot young plants each year before flowering and

ABOVE A well-defined hawthorn, with a nice structure and good nebari (surface-root shape).

ABOVE A *Crataegus* in flower.

ABOVE A twin-trunk-style apricot.

WATERING: Water it every day during the growing season. It likes a misting in hot weather.
FLOWERS: Red, white, or pink flowers.
FEED: Feed it every two weeks in season.
POTTING AND SOIL: Pot young plants every year in early spring and older bonsai every three to four years.
PRUNING: It can be pruned after flowering. It can also be pruned back severely to the stump to achieve a better branch shape, as hawthorns can bud from old wood.
PROBLEMS: It can initially be difficult to keep alive if it was collected from a hillside. It needs to be established in a growing box or training pot for three years before any work is done on it.

Bonsai Quick-reference Table

A BRIEF GUIDE TO SOME OF THE MAIN SPECIES — REPOTTING, PRUNING, WIRING, AND SPECIAL ISSUES TO WATCH OUT FOR

CLIMATE COOL TO WARM

NORTHERN CLIMATES. OUTDOOR — Northern Europe, Canada, the U.S.A., and New Zealand (South Island). In all climates variations will occur, so check with your local nursery or club.

BEECH (Fagus)
REPOT - early spring.

PRUNING - branches winter; shoots in season.

WIRING — midsummer.

BEWARE - pluck leaves immediately they curl open from bud half way.

CRYPTOMERIA
REPOT — mid-spring.

PRUNING — any time, except in winter.

WIRING — mid-spring, to late summer and late fall.

BEWARE — hard frost.

MAPLES (Acer)
REPOT — every 2–3 years, in early spring.

PRUNING — any time for shoots, branches in late winter to midsummer.

WIRING — late winter to midsummer.

BEWARE — wire marks in late spring, aphids.

BIRCHES
REPOT — every 2–4 years, in spring.

PRUNING — trim young shoots through the growing season.

WIRING — summer.

BEWARE — frost.

ELMS (Ulmus)
REPOT — every 3 years, in spring.

PRUNING — winter and summer.

WIRING — winter and summer.

BEWARE — aphid, scale.

OAK (Quercus)
REPOT — every year in early spring (young); every 3–4 years (older).

PRUNING — cut back young shoots through growth.

WIRING — late winter to midsummer.

BEWARE — frost.

CEDAR (Cedrus)
REPOT — every 3–4 years, in spring or fall.

PRUNING — early spring or late summer.

WIRING — late summer.

BEWARE — frost, wire marks.

JUNIPERS (Juniperus)
REPOT — every 4–5 years, in late winter or fall.

PRUNING — any time, but summer is preferred.

WIRING — winter or late summer.

BEWARE — red spider mite.

PINES (Pinus)
REPOT — every 4–5 years, early spring.

PRUNE — and style in midsummer. Bud-pluck through spring to early summer.

WIRING — late summer.

BEWARE — lopho, black aphid, root aphid.

COTONEASTER
REPOT — every 2 years, in early spring.

PRUNING — any time.

WIRING — any time.

BEWARE — avoid overwatering in winter; ground-cover plants are not advised, as root bound.

LARCH (Larix)
REPOT — every 3–4 years, in late winter to early spring.

PRUNING — hard pruning in winter. Do not pluck new spring growth, but cut back to first set of buds on new wood in late winter.

WIRING — winter or late summer.

BEWARE — adelgid, aphid.

YEW (Taxus, also Totara, N.Z.)
REPOT — every 3–5 years.

PRUNING — pluck new growth. Prune branches in summer or winter.

WIRING — winter or summer.

BEWARE — scale, red spider mite.

CLIMATE WARM TO HOT

SOUTHERN CLIMATES. OUTDOOR – Southern Europe, southern North America, southern parts of South America, South Africa, Australia, and New Zealand (North Island). Place bonsai indoors in northern climates during winter.

BUDDLEJA SALIGNA

REPOT – early spring.

PRUNING – early spring.

WIRING – never wire shoots down only to side and up.

BEWARE – delicate bark; damaged bark can die back. Otherwise great for carving.

ELMS (Ulmus)

REPOT – every 3 years, in spring or early fall.

PRUNING – any time.

WIRING – summer.

BEWARE – aphid, scale.

PRIVET (LIGUSTRUM)

REPOT - early to late spring.

PRUNING - midwinter.

WIRING - midwinter to early spring.

BEWARE - wire bite in spring. Cut off some crown when repotting.

BOUGAINVILLEA

REPOT – every 2–3 years, in spring.

PRUNING – late winter to early spring. Then after flowering.

WIRING – after flowering.

BEWARE – feeding high-nitrogen fertilizer, which may abort flowers.

FIGS (Ficus)

REPOT – in spring and fall.

PRUNING – midsummer, as tree heals better.

WIRING – on woody shoots, any time.

BEWARE – avoid overwatering in winter.

MYRTLE (Myrtus)

REPOT – early spring.

PRUNING – trim to foliage pads (topiary).

WIRING – covered wire.

BEWARE – brittle wood.

BOX (Buxus)

REPOT – spring to fall.

PRUNING – spring to fall, remove flower shoots.

WIRING – any time.

BEWARE – does not like lots of sun and prefers semishade/-sun.

HACKBERRY/STINKWOOD (Celtis)

REPOT – every 3–5 years, in late winter to early spring.

PRUNING – winter. Shoots up to midsummer.

WIRING – winter. Only branches, not tips, as tips can die if wired late.

BEWARE – aphid, red spider mite, scale.

OLIVE (Oleo)

REPOT – every 3 years, in spring.

PRUNING – late winter through spring and fall. Trim soft tips.

WIRING – on 2-year-old wood, any time.

BEWARE – scale.

CYPRESS (Sawarra-plumosa etc.)

REPOT – established trees every 4–5 years.

PRUNING – finger-pluck through season. If cutting, spray three times a day for a month.

WIRING – any time, except mid-spring.

BEWARE – internal die-back if not plucked; very dense.

LAGERSTROMIA

REPOT – late winter to early spring.

PRUNING – after flowering/late fall.

WIRING – after flowering.

BEWARE – frost.

PINES (Pinus)

REPOT – every 4 years, in early spring or late fall.

PRUNE – and style in late summer. Bud-pluck in spring.

WIRING – late summer.

BEWARE – lopho (treat with fungicide), aphids (treat with malathion).

CLIMATE HOT TO HUMID

TROPICAL CLIMATES AND AREAS WITH HIGH HUMIDITY. OUTDOOR – GROWN AS INDOOR TREES IN OTHER CLIMATES.

Can be acclimatized in southern climates, e.g., Durban, rain-forest areas of Australia, and all other humid areas – R.O.C., Singapore etc., equatorial America, India.

BAMBOO

REPOT – every 2 years, in spring, or divide root mass.

PRUNING – cut back young shoots to 1cm (½"ï).

WIRING – not required. Prune to shape.

BEWARE – need lots of water.

JASMINE ORANGE (Murraya Pan)

REPOT – every 2-3 years, spring.

PRUNING – anytime.

WIRING – anytime.

BEWARE - bad drainage

POMEGRANATE (Punica)

REPOT – every 2 years, in spring.

PRUNING – after flowering or in winter. Leave 2–3 leaves.

WIRING – late spring to late summer.

BEWARE – avoid underwatering in flowering season and overwatering at other times.

ELMS (Ulmus)

REPOT – every 2 years, in spring.

PRUNING – any time.

WIRING – winter.

BEWARE – aphid, scale, whitefly.

MONEY PLANT (Crassula)

REPOT – almost any time.

PRUNING – pluck out young growth to shape. Cut out tips any time.

WIRING – no.

BEWARE – avoid overwatering.

SAGERITIA

REPOT – every 2–3 years, in spring.

PRUNING – any time, to shape.

WIRING – on young, brown wood.

BEWARE – flowers. Remove them as they weaken plant.

FIGS (tropical Ficus)

REPOT – every 2–3 years, in spring.

PRUNING – in warm periods. If healthy, defoliate in spring.

WIRING – any time on 2-year-old wood.

BEWARE – may dry out between watering in winter.

PISTACHIO (Pistacia)

REPOT – every 2–3 years, in spring.

PRUNING – any time, to last 3 leaves.

WIRING – any time if careful.

BEWARE – remember to mist.

SCHEFFLERA

REPOT – every 2 years.

PRUNING – any time, to shape.

WIRING – does not like wire.

BEWARE – avoid overwatering.

FUKIEN TEA PLANT
(Carmona-ehretia microphylla)

REPOT – every 2–3 years, in spring.

PRUNING – back to 2–3 leaves.

WIRING – any time.

BEWARE – suckers (remove).

PODOCARPUS

REPOT – every 2 years, in spring. Cut off same amount of roots and foliage.

PRUNING – any time. Remove long leaves.

WIRING – on 2-year-old woody shoots.

BEWARE – needs good drainage.

SERISSA FOETIDA

REPOT – every 2 years, in spring.

PRUNING – after flowering.

WIRING – any time.

BEWARE – mildew (treat with fungicide), whitefly, lack of chlorophyll (treat with sequestered iron).

Suiseki, or Viewing Stones

Suiseki have been collected by Chinese and Japanese people for over a thousand years. One Japanese shogun even exchanged a castle for a particular stone that he wanted to have. These stones are so highly thought of that certain old and famous suiseki can sell for the price of a new house.

ABOVE Werner Bub was one of the world's great bonsai technicians. Werner, who lived in South Africa, became my friend. Before he died, he gave me this amazing suiseki. I did not see what it represented at first, but it soon came to me: it is the image of a priest from the waist up, with his hands clasped.

RIGHT I found this huge suiseki while on a collecting trip in northern Italy. It is a waterfall stone, and you can see the tumbling water cascading down the cliff face.

Suiseki are avidly collected by bonsai enthusiasts, as well as suiseki specialists, and, indeed, bonsai and suiseki go hand in hand. The stones often serve as reminders of the places from which they were collected. I often display a bonsai beside a magnificent suiseki as a picture of nature.

When I first started to collect stones in 1972, it was for my fish tank. I discovered that some of these stones looked just like mountains, and they soon began to grace my bonsai benches. I prefer flat-based stones that have been formed naturally, although shaped stones can be cut if required.

Not everyone likes suiseki, but most people can discern a feature of the landscape in the stone. I hope that you can see it some of the examples from my collection illustrated here.

ABOVE Collected from the Eel river in California, I call this suiseki "The Wave." During the 1830s Japan boasted a great painter called Hokusai, whose works included paintings that told the story of great battles, as well as beautiful landscapes and sublime animal drawings. He was the source of inspiration for many of the famous Impressionist and modern painters of the 19th and early 20th centuries in Europe. His set of prints, called *The Thirty-six Views of Mount Fuji*, included one particular print that became one of the most famous images in the world. It was called *The Hollow of the Deep-sea Wave*, or, as it is popularly known, simply *The Wave*. This stone is the image of that print.

Where to Learn More

Conventions are "get-togethers" of bonsai enthusiasts, and are held in most countries. These range from miniconventions of some hundred or so people to massive events of over seven hundred. Depending on their size, most conventions have between one and eight major speakers. The great thing about conventions, apart form the speakers, is the "traders'" stands, as you can find a huge choice of materials, pots, and tools in one place. Conventions are advertised in bonsai magazines in your own country.

The best way in which to find out more information about bonsai is through the Internet. The following websites cover most countries around the world.

Craig Coussins's bonsai pages:
http://www.bonsaiinformation.co.uk.
Email: craig@bonsaiinformation.co.uk

Canada
Toronto Bonsai Society: http://www.hookup.net/~rgoebel

The U.S.A.
There are huge sites accessible through the Internet. Just search for bonsai in the U.S.A.
San Francisco
http://www.gardens.com/club/bonsai.htm
Florida
http://members.aol.com/FLbonsai/mapfolder/bsfmap.html
Los Angeles: Penjing; Ficus Technology
http://www.penjing.com/ficus.html

Bonsai collections
Bonsai has now grown to such an extent that permanent exhibitions of good-quality bonsai are on show. These are a few of the many available.

Canada
British Columbia Canada:
http://www.geocities.com/Tokyo/Garden/1666/
bccollections.htm
Dr. Sun Yat Sen: Vancouver, B.C.
http://www.discovervancouver.com/sun/

Montreal Botanic Gardens Collection:
http://www.ville.montreal.qc.ca/jardin/engl/ejardin.htm

The U.S.A.
Pacific Rim in Seattle
http://www.weyerhaeuser.com/bonsai
http://www.bonsai-nbf.org
The National Arboretum, National Bonsai and Penjing Museum
Washington, D.C.
http://www.Bonsai-nbf.org
International Bonsai Collection, Rochester New York.
http://www.internationalBonsai.com
Eldorado Bonsai, Sacramento.

For a full list of U.S. nurseries, collections, teachers, and dealers:
http://www.geocities.com/Tokyo/Garden/1666/

Index

Page numbers shown in **bold** indicate photograph.

Credits and acknowledgements

The author and publishers would like to thank the following for their contributions:

Bill Jordan – photographs pp. 1, 2, 6, 10, 20, 21, 27, 29, 32-35, 36t, 37b, 70, 72 (4), 73 (3), 93, 117, 126bl, 127r.

Trevor and Fay Yerbury – photographs pp. 63-65.
Trevor has been Kodak photographer of the year for a number of years in several classifications.
He and his wife Faye run the Yerbury Studios in Edinburgh, Scotland.

Ian Baillie – drawings.
Ian is principal teacher of art at an Edinburgh school in Scotland.
He was one of the first members of the S.B.A.

White pine owned by Bill Jordan.
Bill is one of the most experienced bonsai growers in the U.K.,
and has photographed most of the U.K.'s outstanding trees.

Korean hornbeam (*Carpinus turczaninowii*) – owned by Reg Bolton. Pot by owner.

Small-sized bonsai owned by Reg Bolton.

Clump-style maple (*Acer palmatum "Kashima"*) owned by Andy Ritchie. Pot by Gordon Duffett.

Juniper chinensis owned by Ian Stewardson. Pot by Gordon Duffett.

Cryptomeria and twin-trunk needle juniper owned by Ruth Stafford Jones.

Case study on page 56 is by Hotsumi Terrakawa, done in Bologna, Italy, photographed by Craig Coussins.

Other photographs by the author.

The author owns many of the bonsai, the antique pots and suiseki shown in this book. Some of these can be seen at Willowbog Bonsai in Northumbria, England. Other photographs were taken at bonsai exhibitions around the world.